Collaborative
Common Assessments

Teamwork. Instruction. Results.

CASSANDRA ERKENS
Foreword by Richard DuFour

Solution Tree | Press

a division of
Solution Tree

555 North Morton Street

Bloomington, IN 47404

800.733.6786 (toll free) / 812.336.7700

FAX: 812.336.7790

email: info@solution-tree.com

solution-tree.com

Visit **go.solution-tree.com/assessment** to download the reproducibles in this book.

Printed in the United States of America

19   18   17   16   2   3   4   5

Library of Congress Cataloging-in-Publication Data

Names: Erkens, Cassandra, author.

Title: Collaborative common assessments : Teamwork. Instruction. Results /

  Cassandra Erkens.

Description: Bloomington, IN : Solution Tree Press, [2016] | Includes

  bibliographical references and index.

Identifiers: LCCN 2015038715 | ISBN 9781936763009 (perfect bound)

Subjects: LCSH: Teachers--Rating of. | Teacher effectiveness. | Professional

  learning communities. | Group work in education.

Classification: LCC LB2838 .E748 2016 | DDC 371.14/4--dc23 LC record available at http://lccn.loc.gov/2015038715

Solution Tree

Jeffrey C. Jones, CEO

Edmund M. Ackerman, President

Solution Tree Press

President: Douglas M. Rife

Senior Acquisitions Editor: Amy Rubenstein

Editorial Director: Lesley Bolton

Managing Production Editor: Caroline Weiss

Senior Editor: Kari Gillesse

Proofreader: Elisabeth Abrams

Text Designer: Abigail Bowen

Cover Designer: Rachel Smith

With deep gratitude, this book is dedicated to the remarkable, collaborative teachers and leaders everywhere who make schools into learning organizations every day for their learners and themselves.

Visit **go.solution-tree.com/assessment**
to download the reproducibles in this book.

Acknowledgments

This book has truly been a labor of love—or at least a lot of labor. It took far longer than I ever imagined it would, and at some points, I wasn't even certain it would ever actually happen. But there are some who believed in me and the book, long before I was able to deserve their faith. Toward that end, I offer a well-deserved note of gratitude to many.

To Nicole Vagle and Tom Schimmer, longtime friends, sounding boards, advocates of my work, and assessment experts. Your insights have always been shared with openness and grace. Your feedback has always been inspirational.

To Jeff Jones, extraordinary friend, outstanding colleague, and innovative publisher. You believed in me long before I believed in myself. I would not have started the book if it had not been for your prompting.

To Douglas Rife, patient, patient, patient publisher. You offered doses of wisdom and shots of courage along the way. Your grace and patience were greatly appreciated.

To Kari Gillesse, my *remarkable* editor who made this book so much better than it began.

To Claudia Wheatley, a persistent and provocative voice of reason. You more than anyone nudged me forward and worked to protect my time, and I am forever grateful.

To my PLC mentors, Richard DuFour, Rebecca DuFour, Robert Eaker, and all of the PLC associates; and to my assessment mentors, Jan Chappuis, Richard Stiggins, and all of my Assessment Training Institute colleagues. The experts in each group have offered me so many incredible opportunities to spread my wings and grow into deeper understanding of the depth you have brought individually and collectively to the educational community at large. There will never be sufficient words to express my gratitude.

I also owe a note of gratitude to my son, Ethan—a budding graphic designer—for his help with the majority of the graphics found in this book. We learned through this process together.

Most importantly, however, I forever remain indebted to the remarkable educators and teaching teams who have truly and wholeheartedly engaged in the work of collaborative common assessments, most especially Bill Olsen of Rutland High School, Rutland, Vermont, and Susannah O'Bara of Hawk Elementary, Denton, Texas, for sharing your data and examples with me. Educators everywhere have tried the things I have offered, have given feedback and shared results, have helped me understand even more deeply the power of this work, and, most importantly, have inspired and compelled me to finish the book. I dedicate this book to you.

Solution Tree Press would like to thank the following reviewers:

Carie Barthelemess
Director of Assessment
Hallsville Independent School District
Hallsville, Texas

Anaya L. Bryson
Sugar Hill, Georgia

Jan Chappuis
Author, Educational Researcher, and
  Consultant
JanChappuis.com
Portland, Oregon

Sharon Davis
Assistant Principal
Irma Lerma Rangel Young Women's
  Leadership School
Dallas, Texas

Tom Schimmer
Author and Consultant
Tom Schimmer Consulting
Vancouver, British Columbia, Canada

Nicole Dimich Vagle
Author and Consultant
Lighthouse Learning Community
Minneapolis, Minnesota

Table of Contents

About the Author xi

Foreword xiii

Introduction

Doing Assessment Right . . . All the Time 1

Chapter 1

Doing Extraordinary Things 5

  Collaborative Common Assessments Defined 6

  The Collaborative Common Assessment Process 7

    The Preparation Phase 8

    The Design Phase 9

    The Delivery Phase 11

    The Data Phase 12

    The Re-Engagement Process 13

  Collaborative School Improvement 14

Chapter 2

Embedding Collaborative Common Assessments in a Balanced
Assessment System 17

  Assessment Architects 17

  The System of Assessments 19

    External Large-Scale Assessments 21

    Internal or Medium-Scale Assessments 24

    Assessments at the Building or Team Levels 28

    Assessments at the Classroom Level 31

Chapter 3

Working Together for a Common Purpose 35

   Whole School 37

      Collaborative Common Assessments in Action: Whole-School Efforts 38

   Vertical Alignment 40

      Collaborative Common Assessments in Action: Vertical Alignment 41

   Horizontal Alignment 42

      Collaborative Common Assessments in Action: Horizontal Alignment 46

   Across Buildings or Districts 47

      Collaborative Common Assessments in Action: Cross-District Teamwork 48

   Plus One 49

      Collaborative Common Assessments in Action: Singletons, Plus One 49

   Special Circumstances 50

      Modified Assessments 52

      Universal Design 53

Chapter 4

Preparing the Foundation for Collaborative Common Assessments 55

   Establishing Team Norms 56

   Identifying Essential Learning 56

   Developing Shared Knowledge 60

   Examining School Data and Establishing SMART Goals 63

   Mapping Targets and Collaborative Common Assessments 65

   Monitoring Progress 68

      Collaborative Common Assessments in Action: Progress Monitoring 68

      A Culture of Respect 69

Chapter 5

Designing Collaborative Common Assessments 71

   The Design Phase 72

   Protocols for Design Work 73

      Protocol 1 74

      Protocol 2 75

Protocol 3 76

Protocol 4 78

Design Considerations 80

Collaborative Common Assessment Methods 81

Toward a Deeper Understanding of Assessment Literacy 84

Chapter 6

Delivering New Approaches to Assessment 85

Understanding Assessments as a Way to Inform Teaching 86

Collaborative Common Assessments in Action: Teachers Learn in a Formative Context. 87

(Re)defining Assessment 89

Summative Assessment 89

Formative Assessment 90

An Integrated System 91

Delivering Common Assessments Within a Unit of Instruction. 92

Pretests and Post-Tests 93

Frequent Formatives 95

Integrated Interventions 98

Action Research 101

Chapter 7

Examining Data to Improve Learning 105

The Right Kind of Data Conversations 106

A Data Protocol 106

Evidence. 114

The Missing Link 117

Analyzing Types of Errors. 118

Error Analysis to Target Learning Needs 121

Chapter 8

Responding With Instructional Agility 127

Making Program Improvements 128

Curriculum 129

Instruction. 130

Assessment. 132

Better Assessment Designs 133

Planning Instructional Responses. 135

Differentiated Responses 137

Problem Solving When Learning Doesn't Happen .140

Eliminating the Game Playing of Second-Chance Testing 140

Managing Support Between Assessments 142

Deciding When to Advance Learning 143

Motivation 144

Re-engagement 145

Error Analysis and Coaching 149

Enrichment 153

Encouraging Student Investment and Student Voice .155

Expecting Career and College Readiness—All Learners, All the Time. 157

References and Resources 159

Index 171

About the Author

Cassandra Erkens is a presenter, facilitator, coach, trainer of trainers, keynote speaker, author, and teacher. She presents nationally and internationally on assessment, instruction, school improvement, and professional learning communities.

Cassandra has served as an adjunct faculty member at Hamline University and Cardinal Stritch University. She has authored and coauthored a wide array of published trainings, and she has designed and delivered the training of trainers programs for two major education-based companies.

As an educator and recognized leader, Cassandra has served as a senior high school English teacher, a director of staff development at the district level, a regional school improvement facilitator, and a director of staff and organization development in the private sector.

Currently, Cassandra leads a team of assessment architects of the Assessment Center at Solution Tree. She works closely with assessment experts Nicole Vagle and Tom Schimmer and a host of renowned thought leaders in the field of assessment to develop the resources, trainings, and support mechanisms to help educators develop assessment systems that build hope, efficacy, and achievement for all learners in the school setting.

To learn more about Cassandra's work, visit allthingsassessment.info, and follow her on Twitter @cerkens.

To book Cassandra Erkens for professional development, contact pd@solution-tree.com.

Foreword

By Richard DuFour

For many years now, my colleagues and I have asserted that the most promising strategy for sustained and substantive school improvement is to develop the capacity of educators to function as members of high-performing professional learning communities (PLCs). We have also insisted that common formative assessments, created by collaborative teams of teachers, are the lynchpin of the PLC process. *Collaborative Common Assessments* by Cassandra Erkens offers an invaluable asset for educators as they work to become more proficient in using this powerful tool for student and adult learning.

In this thoughtful book, Erkens makes the central point that assessment intent is not nearly as important as the manner in which educators and school leaders use the assessments. The same assessment, she argues, can be constructive or destructive, low stakes or high stakes, depending entirely on how it is used. While there is a great deal of rhetoric in the assessment world on the philosophy and intent of assessments, this book focuses on practical application. Readers will be guided through the entire process, from developing the architecture of a system of assessment through using assessment data to improve instructional strategies and student results. There are four themes that run throughout the book that readers will appreciate: (1) credibility, (2) authenticity, (3) practicality, and (4) passion.

Erkens establishes her credibility through the use of specific case studies with the real names of schools. That adds immensely to the credibility of the data she reports. While many books provide a composite of schools or hide the identity of the purportedly successful schools, she uses public and verifiable data to establish the validity of her claims. While collaborative common assessments are certainly not the only cause for gains in student achievement, she makes a persuasive case that in different schools with different student populations, the same assessment strategies are often associated with gains in student achievement. Another component of the credibility of this book is a superior synthesis of the research. While the author's personal experiences are surely important, she does not attempt to generalize her own work to the universe of students. As her extensive reference section attests, she brings together a variety of other research formats, including qualitative and quantitative studies, meta-analyses and syntheses of meta-analyses. Taken as a whole, the evidence strongly supports the author's claims that the impact of effective assessment depends not merely on the quality of the assessment itself, but on how those assessments are used to improve teaching, learning, and leadership.

Closely related to credibility is authenticity—the degree to which the book reflects real-world classroom experiences. Readers will find extensive quotations from teachers who are directly engaged in the process. These are not authority figures making pronouncements without the distraction of having students in the room. They are real teachers in real schools, who struggle to analyze data, yet persevere through the process. They are professional and confident enough to publicly discuss their assessment results, yet they are also willing to be vulnerable, learning from colleagues and their own students. Another element of authenticity is the author's understanding of the multiple demands on the time of the classroom teacher. Using the metaphor of the architect, she recognizes that assessment is only part of the daily challenge of classroom instruction. Rather than an afterthought, collaborative common assessments must be placed in the complex system of curriculum design, standards, and externally required tests, as well as a host of other demands on teachers who have a fixed amount of time to deliver on a growing number of demands. Teachers who are reading this book will find an empathetic voice in these pages.

The third characteristic of this book is that it is immensely practical. Chapter 6, "Delivering New Approaches to Assessment," is a particularly good example of what common collaborative assessments look like in practice. Just as novelists are encouraged to "show, not tell," Erkens gives the reader not only practical advice but real examples at every level of instruction. "Show me how this works in high school," readers demand. "Show me how this works in an urban environment, EL environment, suburban environment, and so on." These are reasonable requests, and this book delivers. By using illustrative dialogues in a variety of contexts, the author shows readers what successful delivery looks like.

Fourth, this book is passionate. When one considers the words *passion* and *assessment*, educators and students alike are quick to identify the emotions most associated with any sort of tests: anger, frustration, and fear. While recognizing that these emotions prevail among educators, Erkens brings a different sort of passion to the page. In the fourth chapter, she writes:

> Education must be about igniting curiosity, stirring passion, and kindling lifelong intrigue for learners *and* teachers. It's time then for teaching teams to name and claim their vision for their learners, to collectively engage in risk taking and exploration, and to track progress in a manner that builds hope and efficacy for all. (p. 69)

Engaging the full intellectual and emotional energies of students and teachers is at the heart of effective collaborative common assessments. For all the practical advice in this book, it is good to remember that practice without passion is a formula for boredom and burnout.

Credibility, authenticity, practicality, and passion—those are the essential characteristics of what you will find in the following pages. I hope that you will enjoy this challenging and rewarding journey.

Introduction

Doing Assessment Right . . . All the Time

Winning is not a sometime thing; it's an all-time thing. You don't win once in a while, you don't do things right once in a while, you do them right all the time. Winning is habit.

—Vince Lombardi

In a culture of over-testing students, it might seem odd to encourage the practice of designing and using common assessments, even if those assessments were designed to be formative in nature. Aren't such assessments just another level of high-stakes tests getting closer and closer to classroom daily practice with increased frequency? Wouldn't the use of common assessments, whether formative or summative in nature, only generate additional mounds of accountability data *about* learners and teachers? Educators already express concerns about being data wealthy but information bankrupt. Teachers state they feel burdened by the quantity of data gathered by or disseminated to any organization beyond their school, and they openly distrust the quality of those data that repeatedly measure that which doesn't matter and over which they have had little control. Teachers need to be information rich; they need the right information in a timely manner to make *informed* decisions in their day-by-day and minute-by-minute interactions with learners. They require tools that will help them be instructionally agile, able to quickly adjust instruction to respond to learners' needs.

When common assessments are not collaborative—when they are not carefully designed and thoughtfully employed by all the members of the teaching team who require the data to inform instruction—the resulting assessments and the system in which they are embedded could serve as yet another set of "gotcha" tests meant to sort and select teachers and students alike. Unfortunately, many common assessment systems are developed by others (internal experts, external experts, committees of teachers, or a few select teachers) and then provided to the staff who are expected to use the assessments without modification. Such practices happen at every level of the educational system. Though the authors of those assessments profess to support learning with their tools, the truth of the matter is that the assessments are employed by the end users as another tool for *measuring* learning rather than *supporting* learning.

When common assessment systems are not collaboratively designed, employed, studied, and addressed, the following practices can lead to common assessment systems that merely monitor learning rather than support learning.

- State or district officials use the data to qualify (or alternatively deny) teachers for merit pay.

- Educational leaders within a system gather representative teachers to design end-of-term common assessments to be used as benchmarks.

- District- and building-level administrators require a specific number of assessments and the ensuing data be submitted for accountability purposes, but they themselves do not use the data to support teachers in their own continued learning.

- The test developers rely heavily on pencil-and-paper assessments for common assessment work.

- Teachers employ common assessments solely as a pathway to test preparation for high-stakes end-of-semester or end-of-year testing.

- Teachers select ready-made assessments without an analysis of a match to the learning standards, an adequate sampling of items per standard, and a leveling of the rigor involved in the items, tasks, or performance indicators.

- Teachers generate common data without embedding the practice of collaboratively examining and scoring student work.

- Teachers limit data discussions to the numbers before them and do not consult student work to identify the types of errors made in a given assessment.

- Teachers limit data discussions to aggregate cut scores (such as passing the whole assessment at a predetermined acceptable percentage level such as 80 percent rather than passing each target area of the test).

- Teachers generate assessment data so learners can be identified for intervention work outside of the classroom.

All of these practices are alive and well in schools. As a result, the processes of developing, delivering, and analyzing common assessments can feel mechanistic and sterile at the heart of a teaching and learning process meant to be brimming with passion, hope, and possibility. Data not used to ignite passion, generate shared commitments to strengthen the instructional core, and ultimately address the immediate needs of all learners in caring and responsive ways are simply data that can burden—or, worse, hurt—educators and learners alike. Data used solely to measure, confirm, and sort learners into interventions only serve to move teachers and their learners to the point of great frustration, if not the brink of exhaustion and frenzied decision making that can often be fraught with inaccuracies.

Clearly, assessment practices must change if they are to reignite the passion and energy they bring to inform and guide teaching and learning. Yet change in education requires tremendous attention to detail and systems alignment. In and of itself, the work of change is complex and should never be oversimplified; the work of assessing student learning, specifically, takes great care and attention. Oversimplifying or expediting assessment processes for the sake of adult ease can never be justified. Unfortunately, great harm can happen when the management of the assessment process from any level of the organization oversimplifies its complexity, albeit with the best of intentions. In such cases, assessment practice and processes often become applied in uninformed or unskilled ways. For example, educators may label an assessment as a formative or summative assessment but fail to understand how to use it in ways that support student learning. Neither the label of an assessment as formative or summative nor the intention of the assessment matters; rather, it is *how* the assessment is ultimately employed by the end users that will matter most. Simply labeling an assessment to be a specific type doesn't make it so.

To avoid oversimplification and to change assessment practices and protocols successfully, educators must engage others in the new efforts with the following essential components.

- A clear and coherent message on the purposes of the work
- Specific requirements and criteria-based expectations for the work
- Significant skill development coupled with formative measures to ensure mastery of the requirements

Collaborative common assessments and the systems developed to support them require attention and core skills from *each* level of the organization, from central office to building administration to classroom. Many experts have already written about common assessments. By definition, *common* can mean *same* or *shared*, but those two clarifying terms are not synonymous. When common assessments are employed as *same* but are not collaborative in nature, they can be tedious and terrifying for the teachers who use them. Many common assessments are employed as *same*, but they are not *shared* in a manner that individuals and teams maintain collective ownership of the entire process. Often, teams are given time to work together and are required to engage in common assessments and then share responsibility at the point of data analysis and response. Only when classroom common assessments are shared from the design, through the delivery, and into the results of the process can educators truly collaborate in meaningful ways and maximize their potential as a result.

When common assessments are developed and employed properly, as a collaborative, formative system aimed at improving learning for teachers and learners alike, the gains in teacher efficacy and student achievement can be staggering. This book aims to show readers why and how to make these gains through collaborative assessment design, delivery, and data analysis. Chapter 1 explores the nuances of collaborative common assessments and previews the design, delivery, and data analysis phases of the process. In doing so, it shows readers why collaboration is a key factor in all phases. Chapter 2 explains how collaborative common assessments can and should be an integral part of the assessment system as a whole. Chapters 3 and 4 tackle the preparation phases of preparing for collaborative common assessments, from ways to work together as a team to laying the foundations for successful design. Chapter 5 explores protocols in the design phase. Covering the delivery phase of the process, chapter 6 shows readers how assessments can guide future instructional efforts. Chapter 7 assists teams in developing data protocols to examine assessment data in the service of student learning. Finally, chapter 8 teaches teams how to respond with instructional agility when assessment data show that students require re-engagement experiences or extensions.

Together with this book's companion, *The Handbook for Collaborative Common Assessments* (Erkens, 2016), the process outlined here is designed to help teams establish winning assessment habits that will accomplish extraordinary things, including teamwork, informed instruction, and results that restore joy to the assessment process.

1

Doing Extraordinary Things

Collaboration is a social imperative. Without it, people can't get extraordinary things done in organizations.

—Jim Kouzes and Barry Posner

Many variations of common assessments abound in schools and teams. Sadly, many of those variations are both instructionally deficient and "collaboration lite," with little hope of ever helping accomplish anything extraordinary. In other words, the assessment and its ensuing results are viewed as an obtrusive event that generates data but no meaningful information and that is often orchestrated—from beginning to end—with little involvement or ownership on behalf of teachers and their learners, the key stakeholders. In addition, the data are sometimes provided with a prepared digital analysis that may come too late in the learning process to alter outcomes in meaningful ways. By contrast, schools where the work of collaborative common assessments makes the greatest difference house conversations that are instructionally enlightening and teams that are collaboratively dependent.

Collaborative common assessments provide a powerful mode of inquiry-based professional development that seeks to improve student achievement *and* professional practice. For teams to develop the shared knowledge and skills of assessment literacy and instructional agility, they must work together to ask the right questions, explore their own results, and create solutions to complex challenges. If the process is to make a significant difference, teaching teams—and their learners—must remain integral to the design and delivery of the assessment as well as the interpretation of and subsequent responses to the results.

Collaborative Common Assessments Defined

Many experts' definitions of *common assessment* address the same basic ideas: they are given in the same time frame by a team of teachers who share the same students or standards and the results of those assessments are used to make instructional decisions; hence, there is general agreement that common *formative* assessments work best as they allow for making adjustments to support continued learning (Ainsworth & Viegut, 2006; Bailey & Jakicic, 2012; Reeves, 2005, 2006). Much of the writing about common assessments aligns with the work of the Professional Learning Community at Work™ architects Richard DuFour, Rebecca DuFour, and Robert Eaker (2008), who have made it their mission to impact student learning in positive ways, from providing direct instruction for individual learners with specific needs to monitoring for program improvements that must be made at the team and sometimes the school level. Richard DuFour, Rebecca DuFour, Robert Eaker, and Thomas Many (2006) define common assessments to be:

> an assessment typically created collaboratively by a team of teachers responsible for the same grade level or course. Common formative assessments are frequently administered throughout the year to identify (1) individual students who need additional time and support for learning, (2) the teaching strategies most effective in helping students acquire the intended knowledge and skills, (3) program concerns—areas in which students generally are having difficulty achieving the intended standard, and (4) improvement goals for individual teachers and the team. (p. 214)

While teams frequently employ common formative assessments to recognize both students needing support and effective teaching strategies, program concerns and improvement goals are just as important to address.

Education experts concur on what common assessments are, who is involved, and what must be done with the findings (Ainsworth & Viegut, 2006; Bailey & Jakicic, 2012; DuFour et al., 2008; Reeves, 2005, 2006). Heavy emphasis is placed on *formative* common assessments. The guiding premise that all learners can learn and will be successful naturally dictates that opportunities to learn are never done. However, there is a point at which common summative assessments are necessary to certify mastery for students, especially when priority standards have been identified for that very purpose: to ensure mastery for all learners in the agreed-upon essential areas. In addition, common assessments must be designed, delivered, and analyzed in the context of a larger, balanced assessment system. They must be truly collaborative in nature—from start to finish, from teachers to learners.

While the premise behind common assessments begs for collaboration, the practice of common assessments in the field has created variations of collaboration. Therefore, it is important to start clarifying the work of common assessments with the addition of *collaboration* in the title. A *collaborative common assessment* is any assessment, formative or summative, that is either team created or team endorsed in advance of instruction and then administered in close proximity by all instructors so they can collaboratively examine the results, plan instructionally agile responses, analyze errors, and explore areas for program improvement. Collaborative common assessments require teachers' involvement in the entire process from accurate design to effective use of classroom assessment information.

Collaborative common assessments entail a process far more committed to teamwork, instruction, and results than the simplistic, popular notion of providing teams with benchmark assessments and then engaging them in looking at the results together. Collaborative common assessments put educators in the driver's seat and provide teachers with the necessary opportunity to assess according to their learners' needs. The process needs to remain as close to the classroom reality for teachers and their learners as possible.

The Collaborative Common Assessment Process

Common assessments do not require lockstep teaching. Effective assessment practices should never involve rigid adherence to pacing guides, the unthinking application of predeveloped curriculum and assessments, or a blanket approach to instruction. Rather, the work requires an ongoing commitment by teams to create, plan, monitor, diagnose, and respond appropriately throughout the entire process. Beginning at the star, figure 1.1 (page 8) outlines the process teams use when employing the work of collaborative common assessments. In figure 1.1, circles of arrows are used to show the iterative process, direction, and connections in and among the key components. Any shape with parallel sides (rectangle or diamond) highlights the places where teams must function with the degree of parallelism, making team agreements that they adhere to with fidelity from classroom to classroom. This means there will be meetings throughout the process to create plans, check in on progress, respond to findings, and adjust with new plans as needed. The two triangles illustrate the parts of the process in which teachers are providing instruction in their individual classrooms. The triangle—also recognized as the delta, a universal symbol for dynamic change—is used to acknowledge and emphasize the reality that what happens in individual classrooms is unique and ever-changing.

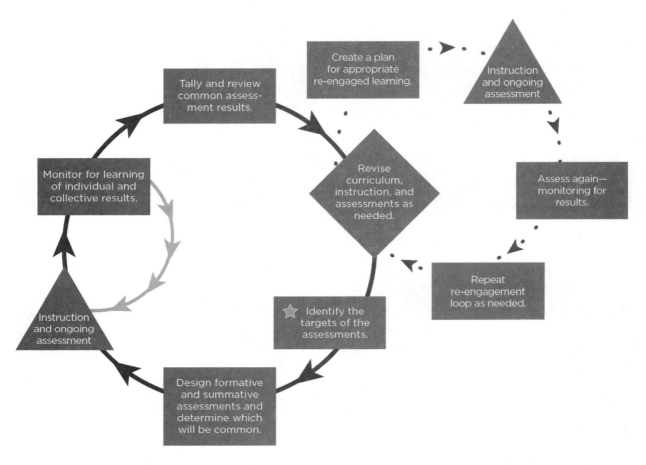

Figure 1.1: The collaborative common assessment process.

The collaborative common assessment process includes four critical phases: (1) preparation, (2) design, (3) delivery, and (4) data. Teams must engage in collaborative conversations that involve critical thinking, problem solving, and creative design during each phase. No phase is more important than another phase, and the success of the team in each phase will be contingent upon the quality of the work and the team members' relentless adherence to the commitments they made to abide by that work in each of the previous phases. Ready-made tools or resources can provide launching pads for planning and discussion purposes in each of the phases, but those tools or resources can seldom be used wholesale, unless the team reviews them and verifies in advance that the tools will align with standards and support team decision making throughout the process.

The Preparation Phase

Working together as a team may be the first challenge in creating, reviewing, and adjusting common assessments collaboratively, but a few critical steps in this phase help educators begin the process with a strong foundation of teamwork as shown in figure 1.2.

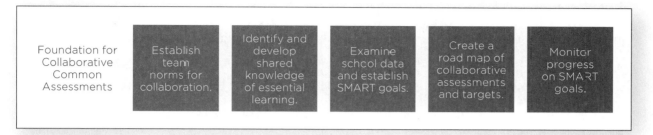

Figure 1.2: The preparation phase for collaborative common assessments.

In the preparation phase, teams will first establish norms. With these protocols in place to guide their work together, teams then begin to chart the course of the assessments they plan to develop. Collaboratively, teams prioritize and unpack standards, explore available data, establish SMART goals, and then create a map of the learning targets and assessments they need to deliver to address the findings and decisions they have made along the way. From here, teams are ready to begin the work of designing the assessments themselves.

The Design Phase

Collaborative common assessments have the greatest impact on student learning and the best opportunity to support teams in managing their work when the summative assessment is designed before the instruction begins. Figure 1.3 illustrates the components that teams address during the design phase.

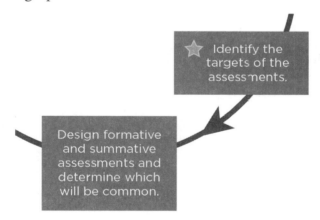

Figure 1.3: The collaborative common assessment design phase.

The design phase begins with identifying the targets of the assessments. As a first step, teams identify the learning targets found in their course or grade-level standards. Identifying and understanding the learning targets is imperative to a team's ability to create an accurate assessment. The targets will dictate the method of assessment required. In selecting and unpacking the standard, the team members have agreed that the standard is so important that their learners will need to master it; therefore, the team will need a common summative assessment to collectively certify that all of the learners have been successful.

Once the standards have been unpacked and the targets are clear, teams proceed to design formative and summative assessments and determine which will be common. In this step, teams begin to map out an assessment plan that serves as a guide to help them make strategic decisions. Every unit of instruction should include a balanced assessment system, meaning there will be one or more summative assessments along with some formative assessments to help frame the pathway to success for learners and their teachers. Not all assessments on an assessment map will be common.

Once a pathway has been delineated, teams need to make decisions about the timing and frequency of their common assessments. Teams who use common formative assessments throughout units of instruction typically find learners require fewer opportunities to re-engage in the learning after the summative assessment because they monitored learners' success all along. So, teams will want to identify a few common formative assessments in their unit of instruction.

The most important part of this step involves actually writing the summative assessment. It is critical that the entire team participates in its development and all individuals clearly understand the expectations for the summative assessment in advance of launching their classroom instruction. All teachers must understand the targets and what quality will look like through the summative assessment in order to be successful in any of the following aspects.

- They are certain the assessment accurately measures the standards and targets.
- They are confident they will generate quality evidence to certify mastery for their learners.
- They are clear regarding their formative pathway to success.
- They can deliver laser-like instruction to support learning regarding the standards.
- They will be able to interpret their results with consistency and accuracy.

Once the summative assessment is created, teams can be very focused and specific in their development and use of formative assessments. Without the summative assessments in place, however, common formative assessments become loose pebbles on a pathway that leads nowhere.

The Delivery Phase

With the assessment road map in hand, teachers enter the next step in their classrooms and begin instruction and ongoing assessment. Although what happens from room to room is never exactly the same, as so many different variables play out while teaching, assessment is an integral component of instruction in all classrooms (Chappuis, Stiggins, Chappuis, & Arter, 2012; Hattie, 2009, 2012; Wiliam, 2011). Master teachers adjust instruction minute by minute as they progress through their lessons. Figure 1.4 highlights the components of the delivery phase of the process.

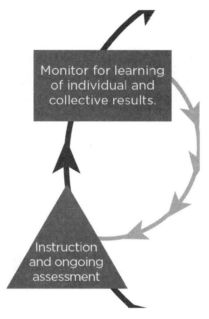

Figure 1.4: The collaborative common assessment delivery phase.

Note the smaller iterative cycle between the triangle highlighting instruction and the assessment rectangle in figure 1.4, which indicates that the individual teacher is monitoring and responding to the results on a more frequent basis, just as the larger team is on a less frequent basis.

The assessments included in the monitoring assessment rectangle range from very informal questions and classroom discussions, to more formal formative assessment checks, to pre-planned common formative assessment checkpoints. In essence, the classroom assessments include almost everything the teacher does to determine where the learners are relative to where they need to be. Teams make individual and sometimes collective re-engagement or intervention decisions during the instructional process to ensure their learners are as ready for the summative assessment as possible. Teachers and learners alike should walk into the summative assessment experience already knowing beyond a shadow of a doubt how they will perform. If the formative assessment process is handled well, summative assessments simply become celebrations of all that has been learned during the delivery phase.

The Data Phase

Collaborative common assessments are the engine of a learning team because they provide the data and evidence that inform practice and ultimately lead to a team's and individual teacher's instructional agility in his or her classroom. Whether the collaborative assessment was formative or summative, teams must tally and review common assessment results and revise curriculum, instruction, and assessments as needed in the data phase. When teachers collaboratively and thoughtfully engage in the data phase, teachers can respond more appropriately to the individual needs of their learners than they may have on their own.

An added benefit to collaborative common assessments over individual classroom assessments is that teachers can generate program data during this phase. Classroom assessments by themselves do not offer great program improvement data because of the unlimited and unforeseen number of variables that may have contributed to the results, whereas common assessments limit some of the variables and provide comparative data. Data in isolation can only form experiences and frame opinions, but data in comparison create information. Figure 1.5 isolates the parts of the collaborative common assessment process that engage teachers in the data phase.

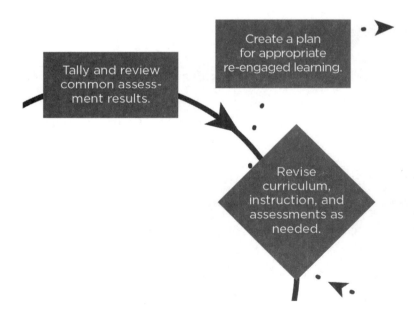

Figure 1.5: The collaborative common assessment data phase.

As teams tally, review, and explore the artifacts and results of their data, they search for key themes, repeating patterns, anomalies, or any other insightful components that will help them revise curriculum, instruction, and assessments as needed to make program improvements. At this juncture, teams use protocols, data templates, and student work to analyze data, conduct error analysis, and make strategic decisions about what comes next in their work.

The Re-Engagement Process

The design, delivery, and data phases are essential components of the collaborative common assessment process. The re-engagement process, however, is not guaranteed. In fact, if the collaborative common assessment process works as designed, few, if any, learners will require additional instruction. Ideally, there will be no need to re-engage learners in the learning following the initial instruction and summative assessments.

The work of responding with targeted re-engagement strategies is pictured in figure 1.6 as the smaller circle, which is a mirror image of the main circle comprising the design, delivery, and data phases.

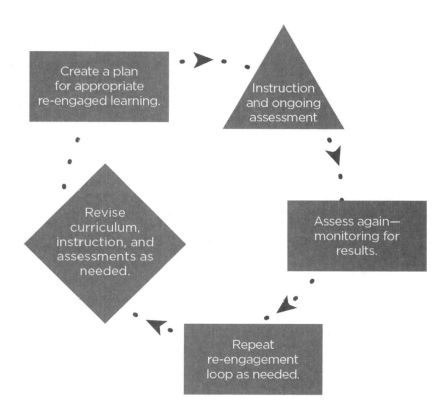

Figure 1.6: The collaborative common assessment re-engagement cycle.

The re-engagement circle is smaller in size to represent the idea that fewer and fewer learners should require additional support, especially if the team worked collaboratively during the formative stages. The process is identical. Once teachers identify struggling learners, they must identify the targets that will require additional time and support, design the next assessments, create focused, alternate, and sometimes corrective instructional strategies and tools to address specific gaps in understanding, and reassess frequently to ensure mastery. The number of times that teams must repeat the re-engagement cycle varies. So much depends on the context: the rigor of the expectations, the background knowledge and skill of the learner, and the degree to which the mastery is imperative for the learner's next steps.

Collaborative School Improvement

Healthy organizations are *learning* organizations; they tenaciously pursue their own internal brutal truths in an effort to attack problems and improve systems (Catmull & Wallace, 2014; DuFour et al., 2008; Pfeffer & Sutton, 2006; Senge, 2006). When speaking of Pixar Animation Studios as a high-functioning and creative learning organization, cofounder Ed Catmull and author Amy Wallace (2014) note:

> What makes Pixar special is that we acknowledge we will always have problems, many of them hidden from our view; that we work hard to uncover these problems, even if doing so means making ourselves uncomfortable; and that when we come across a problem, we marshal all of our energies to solve it. (p. x)

Collaborative common assessments provide the data that help teachers, teaching teams, and even entire schools examine brutal truths so as to respond in creative and inspiring ways.

Moreover, collaborative common assessments provide the vehicle for implementing new initiatives. What is treasured is monitored, and what is monitored is implemented. When teams engage in the work of collaborative common assessments with regard to a new initiative or a new set of standards, they advance its implementation through monitoring outputs. To use collaborative common assessments successfully in the service of implementing new initiatives, teams must frontload their work with the right content, rather than spend endless energies on inputs that may or may not lead to accurate and sufficient outputs.

Educators rightly complain that the field is frenetic with testing for the sole purpose of monitoring progress or lack thereof. In fairness, high-stakes testing evolved in a vacuum of missing information. Education may be overtested, but it remains completely underassessed. As researcher, author, and recognized leader Douglas Reeves (2007) notes, "For too long, the siren song of 'close the door and let me teach' has led to a chasm between classroom practice and educational leadership" (p. 8). There are no industrywide standards that create consistent parameters or uniformly harness the power of classroom assessments to provide instructionally diagnostic information and meaningful achievement data.

The work of creating and employing collaborative common assessments cannot be about generating another set of high-stakes assessments that move closer and closer to the classroom. Instead, educators of all walks and roles must work together to redirect assessment to its "fundamental purpose: the improvement of student achievement, teaching practice, and leadership decision making" (Reeves, 2007, p. 1).

Collaborative common assessments should be based in the classroom, where the heart of learning and daily instructional decision making sits. They must generate accurate, helpful information that is *immediately* and collectively analyzed for the purposes of responding to results in meaningful, targeted, and agile ways. Essentially, collaborative common assessments serve as the engine to the work teams do to improve learning for learners and teachers alike. Team members must share in the design, delivery, and data analysis to maximize their professional learning and truly master their individual and collective craft knowledge.

Embedding Collaborative Common Assessments in a Balanced Assessment System

If you want to make beautiful music, you must play the black and the white notes together.

—Richard M. Nixon

The concept of collaborating sounds pleasant, but it takes considerable effort and commitment on behalf of the participants, and it can only happen when the assessments used to monitor results are carefully embedded in a healthy context and balanced assessment system. Engaging in collaborative common assessments requires systems thinking. When embedded and aligned to the greater context of classroom and district assessments, the common assessment process is guaranteed to intersect and impact classroom instruction, teamwork, school culture, and school improvement initiatives in parallel and positive ways. To maximize the potential of the common assessment process, educators must begin to think like architects with a deep understanding of all the systems involved.

Assessment Architects

Assessment is so much more than writing, employing, and then scoring a traditional test. There is a structure to the overarching system of individual assessment events or experiences. Educators must work as assessment architects—sometimes individually and sometimes in teams—as they structure learning progressions; select, modify, or create assessments; design accompanying tools and resources (rubrics, proficiency scales, protocols, templates, and so on); deliver assessments; score with accuracy and consistency; provide productive feedback; respond in instructionally agile ways; report results; and ultimately build a culture to promote continued and sustained learning over time. Each task is an entire system in and of itself, and a change in one system will likely have an impact on the other systems.

Even though literature about the need to design backward has been plentiful since the 1990s, assessment is still treated as an afterthought (designed the night before the test or two weeks before the final exam) in too many classrooms and schools. This practice is akin to building a house and then deciding that using architectural blueprints might have been helpful to the construction. Constructing a house without blueprints is ludicrous; teaching to standards without knowing the final result in advance is equally ludicrous. Assessment can *never* be an afterthought. Instead, assessment must *lead* the work of curriculum selection and instructional planning. In the house metaphor, assessment, then, becomes the architectural blueprint from which the entire house is built. The standards serve as the specifications that inform the design, the assessment map of formative and summative assessments becomes the architectural blueprint to lead the design work, the curriculum becomes the brick and mortar as it makes the standards a reality, and the instruction—last in the design list—becomes the artistry that makes each house unique: the colors, the textures, the décor. This picture of where assessment belongs in the sequence (standards—assessment—curriculum—instruction) is not new; it has been around since 1998 with Grant Wiggins and Jay McTighe's book, *Understanding by Design*. Education has simply been slow to change practice.

Why does it matter? If educators do not become assessment literate, functioning as architects who put the assessment process in its proper place with attention to detail, they run the risk of any—or all—of the following happening.

- Inaccurate assessments

- Invalid results

- Distrust of the system and the individuals who work in it

- And, worst of all, disengagement on behalf of learners

The costs are grave.

Assessment *is* teaching. To teach without engaging in profound and accurate assessment processes, day by day and moment by moment, is to engage in curriculum coverage. The measure of teaching must be based in whether or not the learning happened. The only way to ensure learning happens is to design the architecture of assessments and assessment processes, from preplanned formal assessments to in-the-moment unobtrusive assessment processes, which scaffold a teacher's way to success. The expression "Begin with the end in mind" is insufficient; educators at all levels of the organization must always begin with ideas on how to *measure* the end they need to have in mind.

It is so important to stop thinking of assessment as a test or a single experience. Likewise, it is equally important to consider teachers as assessment architects rather than parcel out the individual assessment roles, such as test writer or data analyst, on an as-needed basis. Architects are highly trained individuals who must engage in systems thinking with large constructions and intricate details. To create a single freestanding and safe structure, they must adhere to rigorous standards, follow the principles of design, plan for functionality and creativity, and then monitor progress along the way as the building eventually takes form and stands independently.

Assessment architects must create and navigate an entire system of assessments. As contributing experts to the *SAGE Handbook of Research on Classroom Assessment*, Christina Schneider, Karla Egan, and Marc Julian (2013) write, "In a balanced assessment system, teachers use classroom assessment, interim assessment, and year end assessments to monitor and enhance student learning in relation to the state standards and to the state's goals for student proficiency" (p. 61). As assessment architects, teachers must understand how the entire system stands together, supports learning, and verifies achievement.

The System of Assessments

It could be said that collaborative common assessments were born out of a need to better prepare learners for upcoming interim assessments, which then strive to better prepare learners for external large-scale assessments. However, it's time to turn the tables. In a far better approach, teams would generate rigorous and engaging collaborative common assessments that capture the heart and soul of their vision of success for learners. Teams would then use internal and external large-scale assessment data for validation that their local assessment efforts are aligned and equitable in regard to a shared set of standards and criteria for quality. In this model, the paradigm is inverted so that collaborative common assessments become the ceiling, while large-scale assessments become the floor or foundation to ensure quality from system to system. The nuance seems slight—like the difference between teaching mathematics to students and teaching students about mathematics—yet the change in focus is dramatic. The energy shifts from reactive to proactive, allowing for hope and passion to be rekindled for educators.

Still, the process of engaging in collaborative common assessments must involve balancing the entire system of assessments, from formative to summative and from classroom-level to external large-scale assessments. It requires teams to develop assessment literacy as they work together to explore learning throughout the instructional journey in all of the following ways.

- Exploring standards to identify specific learning expectations

- Creating an assessment pathway, rich with formative and summative assessments, and identifying which ones will be common along the way

- Writing assessments or reviewing and endorsing assessments in advance of instruction

- Aligning, modifying, and enhancing the curriculum resources to support students in acquiring the standards

- Providing targeted, responsive instruction aimed at helping learners develop the necessary skills and knowledge for success on the preplanned and preapproved assessments

- Exploring data—formative and summative, qualitative and quantitative—to understand the impact of their craft, identify nuances in results, and problem solve any detected gaps early on

- Examining student work to conduct error analysis and inform immediate next steps

- Examining student work to collaboratively score work and calibrate expectations to be exact and consistent

- Responding instructionally and in a timely manner with meaningful enrichments and targeted instructional strategies to re-engage learners in the learning expectations

- Monitoring for progress and celebrating successes along the way

The entire journey is collaborative and requires the full attention of all members of a teaching team in partnership with the greater context of the school, the district, and even the state. If teaching is less about coverage and more about learning, then the entire process requires that *all* eyes examine current practices in light of specific results, and *all* team members contribute to developing craft knowledge on how to accomplish such a complex, demanding task. No part of the team's journey can be usurped by another part of the organization, such as the district, substituted by a ready-made assessment, or left to the machination of a handy number-crunching algorithm.

External Large-Scale Assessments

Large-scale assessments, sometimes known as end-of-year assessments, should provide the necessary components of measurement, confirmation, and results. Organizations—especially publicly funded organizations with a captive clientele—have an obligation to monitor or measure their effectiveness, to share their findings with their stakeholders, and to address any identified needs as they emerge. Data in isolation shape opinions. A teacher, a school, or an entire district can generate internal evidence that learners are achieving at high levels because they are all earning superior marks, but how do the criteria employed fare against the standards measured on a larger scale? Data in comparison create information. Organizations cannot make quality program improvements without such information.

Large-scale assessments are typically offered annually or bi-annually to help educational organizations identify the proportion of students mastering a given set of standards and then evaluate and address the institutional impact on student learning for the purposes of improving learning for all (Schneider et al., 2013). When large-scale assessments are employed in a criterion-referenced manner against a shared set of standards, educators can use the data formatively to monitor their current reality, explore areas that require attention, and ultimately ensure equity and success for all. Schools cannot improve if they do not have evidence and data regarding what and how well students learn.

The question isn't "Do we need large-scale assessments?" Rather, the question should be "Are large-scale assessments working in a manner that is accurate, supportive, and valuable to the schools and learners they impact?" A single test cannot cover everything, and so tests are used to gather random samples of domains of interest. Consequently, the summary of the findings can help schools and districts monitor for success. Internationally recognized assessment expert Dylan Wiliam (1998) states:

> It has become increasingly clear over the past twenty years that the contents of standardised tests and examinations are not a random sample from the domain of interests. In particular, these timed written assessments can assess only limited forms of competence, and teachers are quite able to predict which aspects of competence will be assessed. Especially in high-stakes assessments, therefore, there is an incentive for teachers and students to concentrate only on those aspects of competence that are likely to

> be assessed. Put crudely, we start out with the intention of mak-
> ing the important measurable, and end up making the measurable
> important. The effect of this has been to weaken the correlation
> between standardised test scores and the wider domains for which
> they are claiming to be an adequate proxy. (p. 1)

Assessment is a tool, and any tool can be used to either build something up or tear something down. While large-scale assessments can be used to help build better educational systems, they have sometimes been used in destructive ways. When the tests are shallow, the results are norm referenced, or the stakes are high, the costs can be significant.

Shallow Testing

The items on any test provide, at best, a representative sampling of what a student knows at any given moment in time. How valid and reliable are the assessments themselves?

> Several studies, using several different methodologies, have shown
> that the state tests do not measure the higher-order thinking,
> problem-solving, and creativity needed for students to succeed in
> the 21st century. These tests, with only a few exceptions, system-
> atically over-represent basic skills and knowledge and omit the
> complex knowledge and reasoning we are seeking for college and
> career readiness. (Resnick & Berger, 2010, p. 4)

Assessments are shallow when they simply test knowledge or basic application through algorithms or procedural knowledge. If the answer to the assessment test questions or per-formance prompts could be googled, it probably shouldn't be on a summative assessment. Knowledge is necessary for reasoning, and it's helpful to check for understanding in the for-mative phases. But by the time learners are immersed in a summative experience, they should be applying the knowledge and reasoning in meaningful ways—to solve a problem or create something new. Summative assessments need to be robust, engaging learners in provocative tasks that require deep thinking, the application of skills, and practice with 21st century–like experiences.

Norm-Referenced Assessments

Norm-referenced tests are employed to draw comparisons. When based on criteria, they are called *criterion-referenced assessments*, and such assessments work in a standards-based system. However, when they compare rank order of individual performance and generate the well-known bell curve, they are called *cohort-referenced assessments*. These assessments do not work in a standards-based system because they measure learners against each other instead of measuring learners against a set of standards. Imagine that all of the learners are getting As, but the rules state that not everyone *can* get an A; now the A is sliced into whose A is higher versus whose A is lower, and the results are reported in a manner that shows who is at the top and who is not. Now the A learner who is at the bottom of the As is recognized as less than his or her peers and is not acknowledged for mastery of the expectations—which is the intended message of the A itself.

The results of schools are often normed as well, creating winners and losers in an accountability system that demands everyone be winners. The practice of norming something (customer service, marketing, scheduling, policies, and so on) is best kept as an internal decision-making strategy; in other words, an organization might norm a common practice within the industry to separate "better" from "best" and then make appropriate decisions about what it can do to improve. But norming is not appropriate as an assessment strategy, especially in a standards-based system, because it labels and sorts *people*.

High-Stakes Assessments

An assessment is considered to have high stakes when it generates significant consequences—positive or negative—for stakeholders. High-stakes assessments are not appropriate in a system of compulsory education: a system in which education is imposed by law, thus making participation mandatory. The concept of *high stakes* is patterned after credential programs in which individuals or organizations must meet certain criteria to earn or maintain licensure (such as getting a driver's license or becoming a doctor, lawyer, pilot, teacher, or any other licensed professional). Unfortunately, the fundamental difference between credential systems and compulsory education is *choice*.

Credentialing works in the system of choice because the risks are lower. First, the individual chose to participate, so he or she is highly engaged during the learning, motivated to succeed, and willing to persist in multiple attempts if needed. Second, the risks are significantly reduced: should the learner fail, he or she is often offered multiple re-testing opportunities. Like the license to drive, the license to practice in a profession is open to prospective candidates on a repeat basis. And, because those studying to pass such exams often have a college degree already behind them, the absence of the licensure may cause initial unhappiness or discomfort, but it will not be detrimental to his or her future opportunities or overall success. There are other career pathways—often within the same field of interest—available. However, in a compulsory system where choice is removed, the difference can be crippling: the risks are too high, and failure eliminates future pathways entirely. The learner who does not pass high school is severely limited in future career pathways, and the stigma is too debilitating for many. Motivation and efficacy—the ingredients for success in life—can be irrevocably impaired when high stakes are applied to compulsory experiences.

All in all, when large-scale assessments are low in quality or are issued in norm-referenced or high-stakes environments, the only changes they inspire are superficial and short lived. Worse, teachers engage in teaching to the test based on specific content rather than increasing rigor or engaging in sustainable, quality instructional practices. Such a system creates visible winners and losers for both educators and their learners. What's left behind is the invisible, residual, but palpable impact of a fixed mindset for both the losers and the winners.

Internal or Medium-Scale Assessments

Though collaborative common assessment work is exclusive to individual teams, the practice of common assessments is not. Schools and districts have an obligation to make certain their learners are ready to perform well on outside measures and are receiving equitable educational experiences and background from school to school within a larger district. Educational leaders at the district level often strive to create common assessments that will monitor progress along the way in all of the tested areas: reading, writing, mathematics, and sometimes science and social studies. Interim assessments, often known as progress monitoring assessments or benchmark assessments, are assessments given over time and with equidistant spacing (every six weeks, end of every quarter, each trimester, and so on) to monitor student progress in achieving standard expectations on a districtwide basis. The primary function of such assessments when developed within a school system is to offer teachers and administrators information about student readiness for upcoming large-scale assessments. The big picture of when the various assessments take place in the system can be found in figure 2.1.

Figure 2.1 is merely an example of a typical system—it does not provide a recommendation regarding what should be happening with specific assessments. The majority of large-scale assessments are given two-thirds to three-quarters of the way through the school year, but there are exceptions. Some states or clusters of states will conduct large-scale testing in the fall as an indicator of student readiness for the upcoming year. The most popularly tested areas include reading, writing, mathematics, science, and social studies, but again, not all states or provinces test the same areas. Figure 2.1 shows districts or boards using similar testing patterns on a more frequent basis than the annual state or provincial testing systems. Building- and team-based assessments are conducted on a much more frequent basis and should certainly include both formative and summative options.

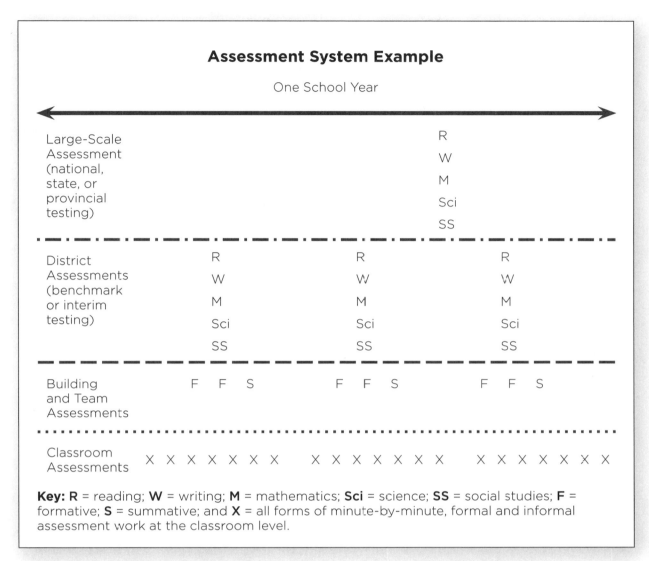

Assessment System Example

One School Year

Large-Scale Assessment (national, state, or provincial testing)		R W M Sci SS	
District Assessments (benchmark or interim testing)	R W M Sci SS	R W M Sci SS	R W M Sci SS
Building and Team Assessments	F F S	F F S	F F S
Classroom Assessments	X X X X X X X	X X X X X X X	X X X X X X X

Key: R = reading; **W** = writing; **M** = mathematics; **Sci** = science; **SS** = social studies; **F** = formative; **S** = summative; and **X** = all forms of minute-by-minute, formal and informal assessment work at the classroom level.

Note: The model depicted in this example is not suggesting that there should be two formative assessments and one summative assessment for each unit; rather, it is suggesting that in a balanced assessment system, there are far more formative assessments than summative assessments.

Figure 2.1: An assessment system example.

When it comes to designing healthy and balanced assessment systems, schools and teams should avoid adopting rules and patterns that oversimplify matters; for example, there is no such rule as needing to use two formative assessments and one summative assessment in every cycle of learning. There is, however, an expectation that teams use *far more formative assessments* than they do summative assessments in their team and individual classroom practices. At the classroom level of the diagram, Xs denote all kinds of ongoing assessments because teaching *is* assessing. The assessments at this level can range from the very informal, overheard student frustration, to the data following a formal exam. Classroom assessments cover all topics, all purposes, and all ranges of methods.

Essentially, figure 2.1 illustrates how assessment systems must be aligned. If the entire system is to work, there must be an aligned flow—from top to bottom and bottom to top, between classroom assessment and outside assessment monitoring systems. Unfortunately, many systems get stuck when outside, large-scale assessments and the metrics they employ to measure success drive the entire system.

District testing, sometimes referenced as benchmark or interim testing, is an important part of the assessment system. It is the only way to ensure there is a guaranteed and viable curriculum firmly in place across the organization. When used, however, district assessments should support teaching teams in their work with collaborative common assessments by providing systemwide validation and by identifying target areas that further inform a team's grade- or department-level assessment work. Unfortunately, because many benchmark or interim assessments are patterned after the high-stakes assessments they feed into, they also fall short of helping teaching teams respond to their data in instructionally agile ways.

Depending on how they are developed and used, interim assessments can make a positive difference in student achievement. Former teacher and administrator, current leadership coach, and author Kim Marshall (2008) highlights the reasons that data from such assessments add value to the organization that employs them:

- Interim assessments can monitor growth from the beginning of a term to the end

- Interim assessments can be more encompassing and require learners to put knowledge and skills together in rigorous and diverse ways

- The results of interim assessments can be generalizable and visible, helping all stakeholder groups engage in analysis and discussion

- Cumulative interim assessments can help track student progress over time

- Results provide opportunities for support systems to be introduced to help both students and teachers

- Results help administrators understand the full picture of how things are going in their building. (p. 68)

It is a given that such assessments can be helpful for program data, especially in larger districts with multiple schools. And it is clear that the use of common assessments as interim or benchmark assessments can have a positive impact. The operative word, however, is *can*. More research is needed regarding the effectiveness of interim assessments. Studies are not yet clear what makes some interim assessments work better than others, which types of assessments work best, whether or not it matters who creates the assessments, and how the test design information is shared or not shared. For example, benchmark or interim assessments are developed and implemented in a variety of different ways.

- Schools, districts, or boards purchase predeveloped testing tools from outside testing companies, such as test item banks, online testing systems, or packaged curriculum-based assessments.

- Districts or boards—often those large enough to house their own assessment division—create their own assessments and strive to adhere to the strictest of standards regarding test validity and reliability.

- Districts, consortiums of districts, or boards bring highly respected teachers together to represent their peers and develop end-of-course or end-of-year assessments. In this case, the selected teachers are advised to return to their schools with generalities but not specifics about the assessments for fear that teachers will teach to the test.

- Districts, consortiums of districts, or boards invite teaching teams to write their own common assessments and then forward those assessments to the department leads or chairs who bring them to the district level where blending and integration processes begin to happen so all of the schools have input, but a shared set of common assessments emerges.

- Districts, consortiums of districts, or boards invite teaching teams to write their own common assessments and submit them for review and approval. In this case, the administrators generally monitor the consistency of the delivery system.

The assessment purpose (formative or summative) is often misaligned as well. In most cases, administrators will tell teachers that their benchmark, interim, or progress monitoring results are meant to be formative in nature, and teachers are advised to respond to the data accordingly to *alter* student success rates over time. More often than not, such assessments end up being summative in nature because of how the results are managed at the classroom level. Even if instruction is altered or additional support is provided, students are sometimes held accountable to all of the scores they generated along the way. Data are used for decision making, but teachers are often marginalized in how much freedom they have to interact with and respond to the results in a timely and effective manner. Worse, students, the primary decision makers when it comes to determining their own success, are often handicapped with pass/fail data that highlight areas of deficit, distort the reality of the specific gaps in understanding or skill, and minimize the assets they bring to the re-engagement process.

Moreover, the use of outside vendors' ready-made tests rarely matches the specific demands of the standards. Speed, ease, finances, and an undeniable urge to pattern local interim assessments after large-scale national or state assessments have dictated that such assessments be measured via bubble sheets, an immediate misfire when it comes to measuring what matters. While previous and new versions of educational standards have been performance based, the selected assessments have not assessed at the levels of mastery required by the standards themselves. The things that the majority of colleges, businesses, parents, and entire countries value most—multidimensional problem solving, ethical decision making, and inventing or creating—cannot be measured in bubble sheets. The data that *are* gathered through such assessments have been predominantly based in content knowledge.

District- or board-level testing is important in designing and supporting an aligned assessment system. Such assessment systems set the standard for internal expectations and guarantee the readiness of their learners for the greater national expectations. As it stands, however, district testing has followed a pattern that educators themselves distrust and dislike. Done well, district testing can make a difference in leading the way to a better testing system.

Assessments at the Building or Team Levels

In a far better model than simply relying on ready-made external options, districts engage teams in courageous conversations about reaching higher and then support them in developing the assessment literacy required to make their vision a reality. With focus, commitment, and drive, educators can create a better testing system. But it will take *everyone*—from all levels of the organization, to all states or provinces participating—to support that effort. Recognized for her work in leading assessment literacy, dean and distinguished professor at the University of Colorado Boulder, Lorrie Shepard (2013) writes:

> The hope, too, is that next-generation assessments will more faithfully represent the new standards than has been the case for large-scale assessments in the past. While the knowledge exists to make it possible to construct much more inventive assessments, this could more easily be done in the context of small-scale curriculum projects than for large-scale, high-stakes accountability tests. (p. xxi)

Developing such high-quality assessments will not happen overnight. Current large-scale assessment designs have established a pattern of testing that makes teachers leery of taking the risks involved with designing alternative assessments. In addition, collectively, teachers have not had the necessary training or experience with designing accurate assessments at rigorous levels and then extrapolating meaningful learning from the results (Stiggins & Herrick, 2007). The good news is that engaging teachers in learning teams to function as assessment architects can build the necessary assessment literacy faster than any other professional development alternative. However, teams *must* engage in the full range of the assessment process with regularity and in collaboration: "Groups of teachers jointly analyzing what's on the test, what's not, and how to stay true to more complete learning goals creates both greater awareness and a shared commitment to avoid narrow teaching to the test" (Shepard, 2013, p. xxi).

Shepard (2013) states, "Teachers need access to better tools, not disconnected item banks but rather curriculum tasks that have been carefully designed to elicit student thinking and for which colleagues and curriculum experts have identified and tested out follow-up strategies" (p. xxi). In the absence of practicing skills, developing a clear rationale, and accessing better tools for developing assessment literacy, teachers will default to testing designs and teaching practices that aim solely at the specific test questions in a manner that elicits recall-based responses.

Leaders oversimplify the complexities of assessment design and use when they buy ready-made solutions. This process opts teachers out of truly understanding the *what, why,* and *how* of assessment design and use. Schneider et al. (2013) state:

> To maximize student achievement, teachers and large-scale assessment developers need to (1) have the same interpretations of the standards, (2) identify the same types of student achievement as evidence of mastery of the standards, and (3) collect evidence using the same types of robust practices in building assessments. (p. 55)

This type of learning cannot be managed through shared documents outlining expectations. Instead, teachers must learn by doing.

In all of their writings, the Professional Learning Community at Work architects DuFour, DuFour, and Eaker have advocated for teachers engaging in the work of common assessments to improve practice at the classroom level (DuFour et al., 2006, 2008; DuFour, DuFour, Eaker, & Many, 2010).

They challenge the premise that outside testing would ever suffice to support teachers in classroom practice:

> The challenge for schools then is to provide each teacher with the most powerful and authentic information in a timely manner so that it can impact his or her professional practices in ways that enhance student learning. . . . State and provincial assessments fail to provide such feedback. Classroom assessments, on the other hand, can offer the timely feedback teachers need, and when those assessments are developed by a collaborative team of teachers, they also offer a basis of comparison that is essential for informing professional practice. (DuFour et al., 2006, p. 147)

Common assessments are integral to the work of professional learning teams. Highly effective collaborative teams focus their energies on addressing the instructional concerns for their classrooms.

Whether functioning as professional learning communities or not, effective teams address the four corollary questions outlined by PLC experts DuFour et al. (2010).

1. What do students need to know and be able to do?

2. How will we know when they have learned it and can do it?

3. How will we respond when students don't learn it?

4. How will we respond when they already know it?

DuFour, DuFour, and Eaker consistently assert that unless teams are doing the work of common assessments, they are not truly functioning as a PLC (DuFour et al., 2006, 2008, 2010). Effective teams use their own data and evidence to adjust, improve, and inform their practice. All four of the corollary questions link directly to the work of collaborative common assessments. Table 2.1 provides the links between each of the corollary questions and its direct connection to the work of collaborative common assessments.

Table 2.1: Corollary Questions and Collaborative Common Assessments

Corollary Questions of Effective Teaching Teams	Connection Between the Question and the Practice of Common Assessments
1. What do students need to know and be able to do?	Effective teams identify the essential knowledge and skill expectations for their learners based on required standards and in advance of any instruction. Teams backmap their assessment plans to align with their standard expectations (see figures 1.3 and 1.4 in chapter 1 as an example). Valid and reliable common assessments are contingent upon a team's ability to develop congruence with required expectations that are answered by corollary question 1.

2. How will we know when they have learned it and can do it?	Teaching teams can only answer this question through the work of common assessments. When teachers review their data in isolation, they frame their experiences and opinions, but the variables that lead to their results cannot be compared in a manner that helps them create information regarding what works and what doesn't work instructionally. Data can only provide information when reviewed in comparative ways against a valid benchmark; otherwise, they are simply random data points. Common assessments provide teams with the evidence needed to help teams answer corollary question 2. Collaborative common assessments are the engine of a PLC because they can drive teams to make more informed decisions regarding their practice.
3. How will we respond when students don't learn it?	Teams require the data and evidence generated from common assessments to answer corollary question 3. Reflection and analysis regarding their individual and collective results combined with collaborative problem solving provide the only means to help teams find the best way to target exact learning needs and demystify complex learning issues.
4. How will we respond when they already know it?	Enrichment, extension, and advancement are proving harder to address than interventions. In all of these activities, educators must help learners who have mastered content and skills to extend their learning. Enrichment does not mean doing more work, helping others to learn something they have *not* yet mastered, or moving to the next chapter. When teams design their common assessment products and processes, they plan for what a true enrichment might look like—one that is engaging and fun while building upon current learning targets that have been newly mastered in challenging ways. When teams design the enrichments in advance of instruction, they can increase motivation and understanding in the following ways. • They clarify even further their own understanding (and that of their learners) of what mastery will need to look like. • They pique interest in advance of instruction by showing learners the possibilities that lie before them if they master the expectations in a timely manner.

Visit **go.solution-tree.com/assessment** *for a reproducible version of this table.*

Team-based common assessments are a critical component of the assessment system. They provide the medium for rich discussion and a pathway into building assessment literacy in a manner that enhances teaching and learning experiences for everyone involved.

Assessments at the Classroom Level

In figure 2.1 (page 25), classroom assessments are pictured at the bottom of the image. This does not mean they are the least important; on the contrary, classroom assessments provide some of the most significant tools, data, and evidence that schools have at their disposal to positively impact student achievement. In the *SAGE Handbook of Research on Classroom Assessment*, McMillan (2013b) states, "Our collective assertion is that CA [classroom assessment] is the most powerful type of measurement in education that influences student learning" (p. 4).

Classroom assessments provide the bedrock of the entire assessment system. An expert in special education and disability policy, Professor Yaoying Xu (2013) observes that "CA can be defined as a process of collecting, evaluating, and using information gathered before, during, or after instruction to help the classroom teacher make decisions on improving student learning" (p. 431). Collaborative common assessments, then, should be designed at the classroom level, leading the team to collective and individual success with clarity in focus, consistency in application, accuracy in interpretation, and equity in responses.

Experts in the field of formative assessment have shared research that classroom assessments—those that are closest to the learners and the learning—provide the best vehicle for supporting learning progressions and certifying mastery (Black & Wiliam, 1998; Chappuis, 2009; Chappuis et al., 2012; Hattie, 2009, 2012; Hattie & Timperley, 2007; Heritage, 2010; Wiliam, 2011; Wiliam & Thompson, 2007). Assessment researchers and authors Rick Stiggins and Mike Herrick (2007) state that:

> Average score gains of a full standard deviation and more have been attributed to the effective use of classroom assessment to support day-to-day student learning, with a major portion of such gains attributable to the continuous delivery to students of accurate descriptive feedback arising from high-quality classroom assessments. (p. 1)

Only at the classroom level can teachers tap into the top strategies that support student learning: clarity of learning expectations, clarity of criteria for quality, and descriptive feedback.

However, classroom assessment can only be as accurate and powerful as the knowledge and skill base of the individual teacher running the classroom. To date, international experts who contributed to the SAGE anthology of research on classroom assessment (McMillan, 2013b) consistently claim that current practices with classroom assessments have missed the mark on the following critical features.

- Using formative processes and tools to promote success on summative indicators
- Constructing assessments that accurately measure what matters
- Gathering relevant data
- Drawing accurate and meaningful inferences with data and evidence
- Diagnosing learning strengths and weaknesses for instructional implications
- Providing feedback that reduces discrepancies based on errors
- Building a sense of hope and efficacy in learners based on results and future opportunities

- Engaging learners as partners in the journey

It has become commonplace for nationally recognized experts to call for a redefinition and better understanding of the practice of classroom assessment. McMillan (2013b) defines classroom assessment as "a broad and evolving conceptualization" (p. 4) that involves both teachers and learners taking an active role in gathering and using data as a means to diagnose strengths and weaknesses, to set goals, to monitor proficiency levels, and to communicate about performance. As a decision-making tool, assessments must gather relevant data that can lead to healthy and accurate inferences regarding what students know and can do in regard to the standards at hand. He notes that the emphasis behind classroom assessment *must* change in that classroom assessment becomes "a vehicle through which student learning and motivation are enhanced" (p. 4).

Teams immersed in the work of exploring accurate assessment design and effective assessment use together can better develop their individual and collective assessment literacy (Chappuis, Chappuis, & Stiggins, 2009; Shepard, 2013). Learning by doing is powerful. Shepard (2013) states:

> What we know about teacher learning, in parallel to student learning, is that teachers need the opportunity to construct their own understandings in the context of their practice and in ways consistent with their identity as a thoughtful professional (rather than a beleaguered bureaucrat). Teachers need social support and a sense of purpose, hence the appeal of communities of practice (although mandated communities of practice may undo the intended meaning). (p. xxii)

Teachers can generalize their learning and findings in group discussions to be transferrable to their individual classrooms "once they get the hang of it" (Shepard, 2013, p. xxi).

However, bad practices are never made better simply because more people are engaged in the use of them. Wiliam (2011), Shepard (2013), and others continue to warn that some obstacles—especially predictable and erroneous misunderstandings in regard to developing assessment literacy—may be too great to overcome just from practicing what was already known. Discovering what works through collaborative common assessments is not sufficient. A healthy, balanced assessment system is in place when districts begin using the data from their own interim or benchmark assessment results to isolate the types of errors and misunderstandings arising in staff's assessment proficiencies. At that point, districts can provide the most effective support through ongoing professional development, dialogue, and internal policy review.

3

Working Together for a Common Purpose

Alone, we can do so little; together, we can do so much.

—Helen Keller

In the simplest view, common assessments can mean the *exact same test*. Many assessments fit that definition: national tests, state or provincial assessments, college entrance exams, interim or benchmark assessments, curricular resource assessments, and grade-level or departmental final exams. Assessments of this nature provide a common set of data related to a specific set of standards or body of information and offer information about how well students are achieving. Not all common assessments must be exactly the same, however.

In most schools, there probably will be very small teams of teachers or teachers who work as singletons (there is no one else who shares their content or grade level, so they have no one with whom to collaborate regarding their specific content or instruction). Small teams and singleton teachers can participate in the work of collaborative common assessments, but it requires a high degree of creativity, focus, and purposeful participation. Teachers should never participate in the work of common assessments simply for the sake of participating. At its core, the goal of *all* assessment activity involves monitoring student learning against a given set of content-specific standards. Fortunately, new emerging state and national standards are perfect for creating and using common assessments because of the emphasis on processes and the clear spiraling of learning sequences:

> A new round of content standards holds promise of providing much more coherently developed learning sequences with atten-

tion to depth of understanding. . . . Recently-developed standards have also attended to mathematical and scientific practices—arguing from evidence, developing and using models, and so forth—as well as big-idea content strands. The hope, too, is that next-generation assessments will more faithfully represent the new standards than has been the case for large-scale assessments in the past. (Shepard, 2013, p. xxi)

Core processes like arguing from evidence support student learning in almost all disciplines. When singletons or small teams of teachers begin by identifying the core processes relevant to their exact content, they can successfully *and accurately* engage in collaborative common assessments. Figure 3.1 demonstrates the various ways that singletons or small teams can use collaborative common assessments.

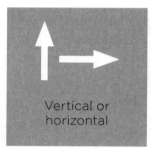
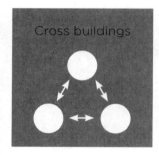

Figure 3.1: Design options for common assessments in uncommon circumstances.

Assessment blueprints also make it possible to create and use common assessments in uncommon situations. With care and creativity, collaborative teams are discovering ways to use the common assessment process to improve their instruction and achievement results. Figure 3.1 outlines the popular ways that teams are using the collaborative common assessment process, even when they do not share content, grade levels, or learners.

The work of assessing learning is serious business. There is a note of caution to this work: teams should never engage—nor should they be asked to engage—in the work of common assessments if the content or processes they would be assessing do not match the content or processes they are tasked with teaching. It is a disservice to teachers as well as an infraction to learners to assess solely for the purposes of assessing. At all times, collaborative common assessments must be used to support, study, and refine the teaching and learning process *appropriate to the standards involved* in productive and meaningful ways. In the service of these endeavors, let's examine the ways teams can work together on a whole-school level, vertically or horizontally, and across schools and districts to best design assessments that support learning.

Whole School

If a school is very small or struggling across the board with a particular skill or process, then engaging the entire school community in common assessments around the same core processes will be helpful. Some core processes, such as technical reading, technical writing, productive group work skills, and the art of persuasion and argumentation, to name a few, are everyone's responsibility. After examining the data to determine the greatest areas of need, teams might reference some of the core processes (which can be found in table 3.1) grounded in that category of need.

Table 3.1: Generalizable Core Processes That Can Transcend Multiple Disciplines

Reading: Literature	**Reading: Informational Texts**
• Main ideas and details • Summarizing • Inference • Evaluation • Literary devices	• Key ideas and details • Craft and structure • Integration of knowledge and ideas • Range of reading and level of text complexity
Speaking and Listening	**Writing**
• Expressing ideas • Communicating thinking • Productive nonverbals	• Text types and purposes • Production and distribution of writing • Research to build and present knowledge • Range of writing
Mathematics	**Social Studies**
• Computation • Problem solving • Communicating thinking • Measurement • Graphing • Mathematical reasoning	• Sequencing • Pattern recognition • Prediction • Argumentation • Advocacy • Information literacy • Global literacy
Science	**Reasoning Skills and Modern Literacies**
• Asking questions and defining problems • Developing and using models • Conducting investigations • Analyzing and interpreting data • Constructing explanations and designing solutions • Engaging in argument from evidence • Obtaining, evaluating, and communicating information	• Creating • Designing • Producing • Information literacy • Global literacy • Data literacy

Visit go.solution-tree.com/assessment for a reproducible version of this table.

As an example, even language arts and social studies teams can support schoolwide mathematics goals in the areas of reasoning, problem solving, and communicating thinking. When schools engage teams in a whole-school approach to collaborative common assessments, leaders must orchestrate time for teams to develop shared tools, provide the necessary background knowledge to all teams, and engage teams in collaboratively designing assessments and scoring student work to ensure accuracy as they monitor improvement over time on their schoolwide goal.

For example, a middle school decided that if its teams used common assessments regarding the process of summarizing in all courses, they could still access their individual content areas. At the same time, they build their learners' capacity to summarize, including the skills of finding main ideas, expanding on key points, and engaging in technical reading or writing strategies. The rubric in figure 3.2 provides criteria for assessing target skills, regardless of the content area.

Engaging in whole-school common assessments can be a great way to help teams launch the collaborative common assessment process.

Collaborative Common Assessments in Action: Whole-School Efforts

Cooper High School officials knew they needed to do something about literacy in their building. While their students mirrored the state's demographics almost perfectly, they underperformed on the state's average for reading proficiency. No one in the high school was trained as a reading teacher, and it seemed virtually impossible that they could do anything about their less-than-satisfactory results.

When educators examined their state data, they determined that their students were low in three areas: (1) identifying the main idea, (2) using textual evidence, and (3) critiquing quality. Teachers agreed that they wanted the students in their own subject areas (music, woodworking, business, family and consumer science, mathematics, and so on) to be successful with those same skills. Everyone engaged students in reading, and everyone believed they could at least impact the students' success if they taught and assessed those three skills.

The staff then made the following commitments to each other.

- We will provide direct instruction in the three targeted skill areas and weave those skills into daily conversation and student assignments.

- At least once per quarter (dates agreed upon in advance), we will give an assessment with our own curriculum addressing those three skill areas.

Student learning targets: I am summarizing when I use fewer words than the author to state the main ideas and supporting details of a text. For it to be a quality summary, I must use my own words in a way that is accurate and makes sense to my audience.

Standard of Performance	4 Exceeds the Standard	3 Achieves the Standard	2 Demonstrates Parts of the Standard	1 Requires Support With the Standard
Topic Sentence	The writer immediately focuses the reader's attention with a topic sentence and piques the reader's curiosity by adding an original or insightful spin on the topic at hand.	There is one clear, well-focused topic sentence that focuses the reader's attention on how the writer will address the topic.	There is a topic, but the reader is left wondering what the writer intends to do with the topic.	The writer has attempted to develop some ideas, but each sentence offers a different idea. The reader is unclear of the focus for the writing.
Summary and Details	The key points align to the topic sentence and are supported with evidence that is vivid and relevant. The writer handles the topic in a manner that is original and insightful. The ideas go beyond the obvious or predictable and offer new information to the reader.	The key points are aligned to the topic sentence and supported with relevant, telling, quality details that give the reader important information. The content explains how or why details are relevant.	The topic sentence is supported with some key points, but either the points are inaccurate or they are insufficiently supported with relevant details.	There are some points shared in the writing, but they seem random or disconnected from each other and from the topic.
Concluding Sentence	The final statement returns to the topic sentence, brings closure to the ideas without redundancy, and leads the reader to a powerful understanding of significance.	The final statement returns to the topic sentence and closes out the writing by concluding the thoughts represented within.	The final sentence is connected to the topic at hand and signals that the end is at hand.	The final sentence is linked to the writing, but it does not conclude the thoughts represented before it and it leaves the reader wondering what happened.
Conventions	Conventions are used to enhance meaning and flow of content. The writer can play with conventions and alter the rules (such as well-placed fragments) in a manner that enhances meaning or punctuates ideas or emotions.	Conventions are used to enhance meaning and flow of content. The reader can move through the text seamlessly and can easily identify the intended message.	Conventions are used, but errors cause readers to reread parts to understand the meaning.	Conventions are attempted, but the application is choppy or inconsistent. Readers struggle to understand the message.

Figure 3.2: Summarizing rubric.

Visit go.solution-tree.com/assessment for a reproducible version of this figure.

- We will always have five questions per skill (identification of main idea, citing textual evidence, and critiquing).

- We will work with each other to write our questions and verify that we are of equal rigor in the level of our questions.

- We will score our own assessments for content and collaboratively review our results regarding student mastery of the three skills.

As agreed, everyone on staff gave at least four common assessments that year, and they reviewed their results together, making collaborative decisions on how best to improve their results each time. In one year's time, the students at Cooper High School went from underperforming to exceeding the state average on the reading test. While the students were still not at the level the staff desired, the staff now understood their own ability to impact the reading achievement results, and the work is continuing.

Vertical Alignment

Collaborative common assessments are vertical when they are used to align a similar content across multiple grade levels; they are horizontal when they are used to align key processes across multiple courses within a department, across multiple disciplines or departments, or across content areas at a grade level. Aligning collaborative common assessments vertically or horizontally requires the use of test blueprints. Vertical and horizontal collaborative common assessments work well with 21st century skills and the new emerging state and national standards. Figure 3.3 demonstrates vertical alignment with the learning progression of measurement and data in the Common Core mathematics standards. While the standards themselves are different, they can be assessed in common ways if teams develop generalizable measurement tools for three traits.

1. Accurate application of data sets

2. Accurate displays of data

3. Quality problem solutions resulting from data

The standards spiral with logical learning progressions, so while the specifics required in the measurement and data standards per grade level will change, the essence of quality work regarding measurement and data will not.

Often, teachers claim vertical common assessments can only work with mathematics because the learning progressions are delineated and clear. The same work can be done with all subjects, however. The work requires teams to clearly delineate and then consistently apply the learning progressions for their individual standards.

Grade 4: Measurement and Data	Common Things to Measure	Grade 5: Measurement and Data
4.MD.4. Make a line plot to display a data set of measurements in fractions of a unit (½, ¼, ⅛). Solve problems involving addition and subtraction of fractions by using information presented in line plots. *For example, from a line plot, find and interpret the difference in length between the longest and shortest specimens in an insect collection.*	• Accurate application of data sets • Accurate displays of data • Quality problem solution resulting from data	5.MD.2. Make a line plot to display a data set of measurements in fractions of a unit (½, ¼, ⅛). Use operations on fractions for this grade to solve problems involving information presented in line plots. *For example, given different measurements of liquid in identical beakers, find the amount of liquid each beaker would contain if the total amount in all the beakers were redistributed equally.*

Source: NGA & CCSSO, 2010b.

Figure 3.3: Example of vertical alignment for common assessments in mathematics.

Collaborative Common Assessments in Action: Vertical Alignment

At Innovation Elementary, a K–5 building, the staff acknowledged that while their scores were low in mathematics, they were observing a steady increase in student achievement, and they felt confident that progress was being made with marked improvement over time. However, their reading scores were low and stagnant, as no observable changes had happened within the last five years. Each team was charged with identifying SMART (strategic and specific, measurable, attainable, results oriented, and time bound) goals for improvement in the area of reading.

Teachers in all grades decided to work on the reading skill of making connections in three categories: text to self, text to the world, and text to text. To begin, the teams collaboratively developed a rubric for making connections in each of the three categories when reading. They tried to write the rubric so that it would be usable in the following ways:

- Through both fiction and nonfiction texts
- Across different grade levels

- Across different levels of text complexity

- Across different content (science, social studies, language arts, and so on)

Once the rubric was developed, each grade level set about creating assessments that would use the rubric the staff had just agreed to use. Even though they offered their students different materials with different levels of difficulty, the teams agreed to gather and collaboratively evaluate their results, making sure their learners had the necessary skills for making connections.

This approach allowed everyone in those grade levels, including the specialists, to help the learners cite textual evidence and make inferences. It also helped the specialists link reading directly to their own content. For example, the music teacher and the art teacher could both engage learners in assessments that involved making connections between their content-specific work and the grade-level teams' overall reading goal.

Horizontal Alignment

Collaborative common assessments can be horizontally aligned (across different content areas) as well. In this scenario, teams tap into some common strategic targets—those that are most important to their entire grade level, department, or school's success—and address achievement gaps.

To design collaborative common assessments horizontally, teams must first identify the core skills or processes that will be practiced throughout their entire curriculum. Once those components are named, the teams can create a consistent set of rubrics for assessing the standards across their various courses whenever they are engaged in using performance assessments or constructed-response assessments.

When teams engage in creating assessment blueprints, they can even do the work of vertical common assessments with the traditional selected-response items. Assessment blueprints are used to map out the structure of a test, control for assessment content, and enhance content rigor and validity in the traditional pencil-and-paper testing formats (Wright, 2008). Assessment blueprints involve using a table to map the content of the test with two different dimensions—one strategic and one specific target area. An assessment blueprint can have any number of columns or rows. The intersecting cells between the specific targets and the strategic targets show the number of test items that will fit within that corresponding cell. Figure 3.4 provides an example of a test blueprint.

	Strategic Target	Strategic Target	Strategic Target
Specific Target	Number of questions that will link the strategic and specific targets together	3 questions	4 questions
Specific Target	4	2	2

Sources: Stiggins, 2001; Wright, 2008.

Figure 3.4: Assessment blueprint example.

Once the team members have identified their strategic or shared processes, they can develop assessment blueprints that will enable them to use selected-response assessment structures in collaborative common assessment processes where the specific targets will not be similar but the strategic targets will.

Imagine, for example, that a secondary social studies department decides to implement the new College, Career, and Civic Life (C3) Framework for Social Studies State Standards. Specifically, the department decides to focus all of its work, whether in civics, history, economics, or geography, on these core skills (National Council for the Social Studies, 2013, p. 12):

- Developing questions and planning inquiries
- Gathering and evaluating sources
- Developing claims and using evidence
- Communicating and critiquing conclusions
- Taking informed action

Naming core processes (strategic targets) empowers teams to implement the standards through the collaborative common assessment process. It will require teams to work carefully, ensuring that every subject area and course is activating and interpreting the core skills the same way. For example, in the case of the social studies department, the eighth-grade history teacher has state standards regarding the American Revolution in her course. She created learning targets (specific targets) to meet the demands of her standard.

Unit: Political Unrest and the American Revolution, 1763 Through Mid-1791

Standard: Students will demonstrate an understanding of the causes and consequences of the American Revolution and its role in shaping the United States today.

Learning Targets:

1. I can analyze the leadership traits and skills of the key players in the American Revolution.

2. I can identify and apply the principles of the Declaration of Independence to scenarios that address issues of inalienable rights and self-evident truths.

3. I can describe and trace the issues and events that led to the American Revolution and resulted in our independence from Britain.

She decides to engage in a common formative assessment with her seventh-grade geography colleague. Both fully understand that the demands of the C3 Framework require learners to create products and engage in taking action, so they agree to ensure that learners grasp necessary skills to attain those expectations. The history teacher decides to use a test to monitor the learners' progress, and creates a blueprint for a typical paper-and-pencil test to check for learners' readiness to advance to projects requiring those skills.

Figure 3.5 highlights the test blueprint that the teacher creates for her history assessment.

	Developing Claims	Using Evidence	Critiquing Conclusions	Total Number of Test Questions
Key Players	3	4	3	10
Declaration of Independence	7	3	7	17
Causes and Consequences	4	5	4	13
Total Number of Test Questions	14	12	14	40 Questions Total

Figure 3.5: Assessment blueprint for American Revolution unit test.

The seventh-grade geography teacher has a different content standard (specific targets), but he shares the same processes (strategic targets) from the Social Studies C3 Framework. While his state standards pertain to U.S. geography, he also translates his standard into student-friendly learning targets.

Unit: The Great Western Expedition

Standard: Students will describe significant geographic characteristics of the many regions of the United States.

Learning Targets:

1. I can gather and compare information about a place by engaging a variety of geographic representations, such as political, physical, and topographic maps, and globes from different eras.

2. I can describe the movement of people, ideas, diseases, and products in the United States.

3. I can identify the causes and consequences of historical issues in the United States, such as the expansion of markets, the urbanization of the developing world, the consumption of natural resources, and the extinction of species.

So, both common assessment test blueprints look similar in terms of strategic targets, but each assesses a different specific target. Figure 3.6 illustrates the geography teacher's test blueprint for his collaborative common assessment.

	Developing Claims	Using Evidence	Critiquing Conclusions	Total Number of Test Questions
Geographic Representations	3	4	3	10
Concept of Movement	4	5	4	13
Causes and Consequences	7	3	7	17
Total Number of Test Questions	14	12	14	40 Questions Total

Figure 3.6: Assessment blueprint for U.S. geography unit test.

When using horizontally constructed common assessments, the weight (number of questions) assigned to the specific targets can flex, but the weight assigned to the specific targets should remain consistent for the teams to have comparable data regarding the strategic targets. It is important that the teachers examine each other's assessment items in advance so as to guarantee they employ a consistent level of rigor and the strategic targets are accurately represented in the challenges before the learners engage in the assessment.

Common Core standards for mathematics and English language arts, Next Generation Science Standards, and the Social Studies C3 Framework all lend themselves to the work of collaborative common assessments. However, teams should not engage in the work simply because it's fashionable. Ultimately, they must engage in the work to improve their own teaching and learning processes. The content and processes teachers assess *must* remain pertinent to their standards and meaningful to their instruction in the classroom. To be clear, assessment must always operate in service to the learner about the learning; it is an abuse of the learner and a failure of the system if the learner is tasked with participating in an inappropriate, inaccurate assessment for the sake of a contrived system that benefits only the educators administering it.

Collaborative Common Assessments in Action: Horizontal Alignment

Redding High School is small, and there are only one or two teachers per grade level. The ninth-grade social studies and science teams decided to address the English language arts (ELA) standards for technical subjects together. To begin, they isolated the ways they could measure their individual content in common ways. Technical subjects involve technical reading that includes the use of charts, graphs, and data analysis. The team decided to isolate three aspects of examining technical information (concept accuracy, perspective, and implications) and to create rubrics (as shown in figure 3.7) using those aspects to explore analyzing data, reasoning and evidence with data, and comparative perspectives when handling data.

	Concept Accuracy	Perspective	Implications
Quantitative or technical analysis (content specific)	Rubric		
Reasoning and evidence to support the author's claims (content specific)	Rubric		
Compare and contrast treatments of the same topic (content specific)	Rubric		

Figure 3.7: Redding High School's rubrics for assessing technical information.

Then, the teams got busy identifying their individual content areas.

In history I, students examine the historical and intellectual origins of the United States during the Revolutionary War and Constitution eras. Students study the basic framework of American democracy and the basic concepts of American government, as well as America's westward expansion, the establishment of political parties, economic and social change, sectional conflict, the Civil War, and Reconstruction.

The team's work would span multiple units, but the social studies teachers decided to begin with the unit on the Revolutionary War. They wanted to assess the following Common Core State Standards for English Language Arts & Literacy in History/Social Studies, Science, and Technical Subjects (NGA & CCSSO, 2010a).

- **RH.9–10.7:** Integrate quantitative or technical analysis (such as charts or research data) with qualitative analysis in print or digital text.

- **RH.9–10.8:** Assess the extent to which the reasoning and evidence in a text support the author's claims.

- **RH.9–10.9:** Compare and contrast treatments of the same topic in several primary and secondary sources.

They planned to use the common rubric tools they had developed with the science and technical subjects teachers.

The grade 9 earth and science teachers engage their learners in hands-on laboratory and field experiences that include reading and interpreting maps, keys, and satellite, radar, and telescope imageries; using satellite and radar images and weather maps to illustrate weather forecasts; using seismic data to identify regions of seismic activity; and using data from various instruments that are used to study deep space and the solar system, as well as inquiry skills.

The team decided to start with the following standards (NGA & CCSSO, 2010b).

- **RST.9–10.7:** Translate quantitative or technical information expressed in words in a text into visual form (such as a table or chart) and translate information expressed visually or mathematically (for example, in an equation) into words.

- **RST.9–10.8:** Assess the extent to which the reasoning and evidence in a text support the author's claim or a recommendation for solving a scientific or technical problem.

- **RST.9–10.9:** Compare and contrast findings presented in a text to those from other sources (including their own experiments), noting when the findings support or contradict previous explanations or accounts.

Across Buildings or Districts

The third way that small teams or singleton teachers can engage in common assessments is to join up with like educators from other schools or educational organizations. In the cross-building or cross-district option, art teachers in one school join up with art teachers in one or more of the other schools that may be in the same district or even in neighboring districts.

In a large urban high school district, the various buildings want to make sure they are tracking together. Each department conducts its own local common assessments, but the department chairs from each high school work together across the district to make sure that their end-of-semester assessments will be consistent from course to course and school to school. They each bring their own examples of the common assessments they have been using in their building, and then together, in cross-district formation, they build their districtwide end-of-semester common assessments. They return to their own buildings and share the planned assessments with their peers.

In one rural school district, the schools are far apart, and it takes too long for teachers to drive to the other school. The teams meet electronically, conducting a Google Hangout while using Google Docs. In that setting, they can design assessments together, interpret results, make re-engagement plans, and so on.

With today's technology, this is easy to accomplish through virtual meetings and online collaborative tools with which teams can readily share data and create common tools. In this manner, alternative high schools can work with traditional high schools, and so on.

Collaborative Common Assessments in Action: Cross-District Teamwork

In Islo School District, there are three middle schools. Each middle school has one band director who teaches grades 6 through 8. Unfortunately, it did not always work out that the collaborative time of one building would line up with the collaborative time of another building. Therefore, meeting during collaborative time was impossible, and the administration requested that the three instrumental music teachers find people within their own buildings with whom to collaborate, such as the vocal music teachers or the art teachers.

The team of three instrumental music teachers was adamant that the best way to improve in teaching band was to talk with other band teachers. The three teachers planned creative ways to use their assigned collaborative time electronically (meeting via email) and to also reallocate time so they could meet on their own. They sought permission to trade time by taking ten minutes off the end of each day and then adding forty minutes to the beginning of the first Wednesday of each month, and committed to gathering evidence that their collaborative time was as important and as beneficial as any other team's time within the normal schedule. Once they launched, they identified their eight to ten big ideas for each grade in band and generated the assessments and rubrics to score student work. It took a full year before they were able to convince the administration to revamp their schedules so that they could meet on Friday mornings at least twice a month. However, the three teachers believe their efforts were well worth the outcome. Persevering and providing evidence paid off.

These teachers have proof that they are doing more as a team to help their learners achieve in instrumental music than they had ever been able to do on their own.

Plus One

Finally, there is a fourth way that very small teams, singleton teachers, or even groups of singleton teachers can participate in or support the process of collaborative common assessments—they opt in as a plus one. In this model, a singleton teacher or a few singleton teachers join in with the work of another team or several teams of general education teachers. They do so because they choose to be part of improving student achievement through a venue that involves job-embedded staff development. Teachers engaged in this work continually express their belief that all subject matter is core to developing literacy and central to every learner's success. In this scenario, teachers validate their curriculum as an integral part of the school's improvement efforts to impact reading, writing, and math literacy. They no longer wish to be the curriculum that gets cut when learners need additional time and support with literacy. They choose to be part of the solution.

Collaborative Common Assessments in Action: Singletons, Plus One

Independence Elementary is a K–6 building with a single physical education (PE) teacher, Bill. It is the only elementary school in the district, and there are no other districts in the immediate vicinity with whom the PE teacher can collaborate. When he started teaching, Bill knew that some students only learn through movement, and his classes provided them with an opportunity to move during the day. He wanted to engage in the work of collaborative common assessments because he saw his peers gaining instructional insights as well as a strong sense of camaraderie.

In the first year, he asked the teachers at each grade level to share their mathematics facts and their vocabulary words for the upcoming week. He wove the grade-level-specific mathematics facts into his classroom warm-up exercises and the grade-level-specific vocabulary words into his cool-down exercises. Students were tasked with creating a catchy jingle or cadence through which they recited the week's learning, much like a marching troupe might. Within the first month, teachers from each grade level approached Bill to express their surprise at the effectiveness of his work. They had evidence that their learners were benefitting from the frequent recitations and the cadences they played in their heads on testing day.

Bill was thrilled that he was contributing to the students' success schoolwide, but he still felt like he was not tackling the content that mattered. In the second year of his efforts, he approached the first-grade teachers and asked if he could be part of their team for the upcoming year. The first-grade team was baffled. While the teachers wanted to involve Bill and they knew their learners would benefit, they had no idea *how* they would go about doing that work. But Bill knew. He'd been planning options all along. He asked the team to share with him three of its core verbs for its reading work, and then he provided examples of how he could engage learners in exploring those verbs in his classroom. The team offered Bill the following reading verbs, as shown in figure 3.8.

Grade 1 reading verb ideas	Bill's response to the reading verb in action when learners are engaged in a PE classroom
Compare	Compare the results that occur when we throw the ball overhanded, underhanded, fast, slow, and so on.
Predict	Predict what will happen if we set goals to run faster and farther each day and then monitor progress along the way.
Infer	Make inferences about alertness levels in the regular classroom following low-impact, medium-impact, and high-impact PE activities. Track progress over time to evaluate inferences.

Figure 3.8: Collaborating as a singleton at Independence Elementary School.

Bill told the team teachers that if they would just give him the main reading verbs in advance, he would commit to engaging the grade 1 learners in exploring the verbs through his classroom. He wanted to know if his contributions improved their assessment results after his engagement in the first few units. The team teachers agreed to try it and to invite him into the design work for their collaborative common assessments as well as their examination of student work. In turn, Bill committed to sharing his findings so they could compare notes regarding the first-grade learners' understanding of the core reading processes in and beyond the reading classroom.

As DuFour, DuFour, and Eaker (2008) are quick to assert, the best way to improve instruction and assessment practices is to engage collaborative teams of teachers to examine and refine their craft through their own results. The traditional practice of teacher observation can fall seriously short of supporting teacher growth if the observer or evaluator has limited knowledge of the content expertise required. Teams deepen content knowledge and refine instruction and assessment practices when they work to develop shared knowledge with a critical eye and a commitment to mastery.

Special Circumstances

It is often assumed that teachers who work with learners requiring special services, such as special education students or English learners, should be exempt from engaging in collaborative common assessments. Should their learners even have to participate in common assessments? If assessment is used to support learning, then the answer is a resounding *yes*:

> While students with special needs have an individualized education program (IEP) that may differ from the general education curriculum in learning targets, the goal of data collection similarly is to improve students' learning by informing teachers to make appropriate decisions in the progress monitoring process. (Xu, 2013, p. 431)

Critical instructional decisions must be made based on local evidence gathered through formal and informal assessment processes, teachers' knowledge of and experience with the learners' strengths and limitations, and the resulting collective reasoning within the team. As Xu (2013) notes, "It is essential that the general education teacher, collaboratively with the special education teacher and other team members, make reflective decisions and improve the learning of both students with or without disabilities" (p. 431). Every expert at the table must be able to support every struggling learner in the classroom. Committed to the work of helping schools create successful intervention systems to support learning, authors Austin Buffum, Mike Mattos, and Chris Weber (2012) assert that special education teachers have expertise that can benefit general education teachers and students, while general education teachers have specific content knowledge that can benefit special education teachers and students. Challenges with learning require an "all hands on deck" approach. Siloed services cannot be tolerated. Everyone must be monitoring for learning, and common assessments provide systemwide and consistent monitoring tools.

The issue isn't whether or not to use common assessments; rather, the issue is how to use them appropriately with learners who are not on the traditional path. The experts in English learning (EL) and special education concur that *all* learners should enjoy the benefits of a group of wise educators monitoring their progress over time.

- "Meeting the needs of all students, whether prereferral or after a student has an IEP, is the responsibility of all educators at all times" (Buffum et al., 2012, p. 195).

- "The IDEA [Individuals with Disabilities Education Act] requires that all students with disabilities have the rights to receive an unbiased and nondiscriminatory evaluation conducted by a multidisciplinary team to determine these students' educational needs" (Xu, 2013, p. 431).

- "One of the most important new provisions added to IDEA 1997 was that the law required 'whenever appropriate' that general education classrooms should be used for children with special needs, recognizing that most kids with disabilities spent all or most of their time in general education settings" (Xu, 2013, p. 431).

- According to the Center for Equity and Excellence in Education, "[EL] students should be evaluated with appropriate and valid assessments that are aligned to state and local standards and take into account language acquisition stages and cultural backgrounds of students" (Almeida, 2007, p. 155).

- "One of the most important revelations stemming from brain research is that there are no 'regular' students. The notion of rigid categories of learners—smart/not smart, disabled/not disabled, regular/irregular—is an unrealistic oversimplification. By categorizing students in this way, we focus on single characteristics while missing many subtle and important qualities. The truth told by brain research is that each student brings a unique assortment of strengths, challenges, and preferences into the learning environment" (Dolan & Hall, 2001, p. 22).

Precisely because classroom assessment differs from high-stakes or standardized tests, teachers must find ways to engage all learners—especially nontraditional learners—in the collaborative common assessment process. Collective focus and shared commitment are required when it comes to addressing learning challenges, whether that challenge is demographic based or ability based. To monitor progress effectively, teachers and learners alike require access to the most valuable evidence closest to the instructional decision-making process.

Modified Assessments

Just as with any assessment, it is possible to modify a common assessment to meet the IEPs, 504 plans, or EL requirements for all learners. To begin, it's important to be clear about *what* is being assessed. Second language learners might be able to complete the mathematics if language weren't a barrier. Likewise, struggling readers may experience difficulty with reading the actual words, but their ability to comprehend and draw conclusions can remain intact.

Teachers have an obligation to understand what they are assessing long before they strive to modify the assessment to meet the needs of individual learners. Once the learning targets of the common assessment are clear and each individual's learning needs are articulated, the team members can create modified versions of the assessment and still create for themselves the ability to review the data and make informed instructional decisions that are target *and* learner specific (Dolan & Hall, 2001).

Universal Design

Instead of modifying individual assessments to meet the needs of individual learners, the best option is to create assessments that meet the standards of universal design and can be readily accessible to all learners. All learners have a better opportunity to engage during the learning process and then share their learning at a deeper conceptual level when they are immersed in assessments that move beyond sharing recall-level expectations (such as constructed or performance-based assessments). Almeida (2007) notes that:

> authentic or performance-based assessment instruments yield more accurate results with English language learners than traditional assessments, regardless of whether they are used to collect summative data (for a status report) or formative data (to affect learning). The results of these authentic assessments tend to be indicative of students' conceptual understanding of the concept or skill. (p. 153)

Her assertion has value beyond the needs of ELs; teachers can better grasp the conceptual understanding and skills of all learners when engaging them in authentic assessments. And such assessments more readily align with the demands of 21st century skills and the requirement of increased rigor in current testing practices.

All assessment designs and methods must promote a continued increase in rigor and relevance for all learners. A framework called universal design (UD) was developed in an effort to increase accessibility to all assessments, for all learners:

> Using this framework, tests can be designed for the broadest group of test takers without the need to accommodate specific subpopulations. The National Center for Educational Outcomes (Thompson et al., 2002) adapted the original UD principles into the following assessment features: (1) inclusive assessment population; (2) precisely defined constructs; (3) accessible, nonbiased items; (4) amenable to accommodations; (5) simple, clear, and intuitive instructions and procedures; (6) maximum readability and comprehensibility; and (7) maximum legibility. Thus, in terms of testing, the objectives of UD are to remove all item features that interfere with the measurement of the construct—that is, those contributing construct-irrelevant variance—and extend access to all test takers at all levels of the construct. (Rodriguez & Haladyna, 2013, p. 303)

The goal in writing universal design-based assessments is to build in methods that will allow all learners equitable access to the content at hand, rather than to create a single assessment that works within tight constraints to meet the needs of all (Almond et al., 2010). Ultimately, assessment is a process that we must do with and for our learners—not to them.

Preparing the Foundation for Collaborative Common Assessments

Before anything else, preparation is the key to success.

—Alexander Graham Bell

It would be wrong to send teams off to employ common assessments—whether pre-endorsed or collaboratively developed—without setting the context and providing a firm foundation for the work. In an accountability-rich culture, it is readily assumed that any data generated are visible and therefore available for decision makers. When the stakes are too high, the process will not work to invite innovation and encourage practice improvement if it is not managed well.

Figure 4.1 frames the foundation by outlining the components that are within a team's control and that must be part of the team's work *before and during* the process of designing and employing collaborative common assessments.

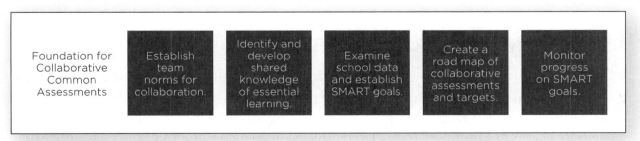

Figure 4.1: The preparation phase for collaborative common assessments.

Collaborative common assessments are only going to be as meaningful and successful as the foundation on which they are built. The work requires teachers to consider themselves learners and active researchers regarding their own craft knowledge. It also requires the leaders around them to adopt a very formative stance as they ask the teachers to engage with students. In other words, mistake making and failing are going to be part of the learning process. Teams must create systems of safety and formalize parameters and guidelines for the work to support the teams' ongoing learning by doing.

Establishing Team Norms

If collaborative common assessments are truly going to be collaborative in nature, then it is important for teams to launch their efforts from a base of trust. In the past, educators have invoked trust as a hands-off policy: *I trust her to go into her classroom, use her professional judgment, and do great work for students.* In reality, trust—especially in interdependent and synergistic situations—requires attending to culture and details with intentionality. It simply cannot be left to chance, but must instead be orchestrated, practiced, and discussed. Trust cannot be manufactured, but the conditions can be created and monitored to support a natural outgrowth of trust.

As a starting point, teams must establish team norms. Unfortunately, many team norms look like professional courtesies (show up on time, agree to participate, turn off cell phones, and so on), and they do little to ensure that the conditions for trust are built. Such norms demonstrate professional standards and should be part of the given culture rather than written commitments to one another (Erkens & Twadell, 2012). To support the deep levels of collaboration required in collaborative common assessments, teams will need to develop norms that serve as collective promises to hold each other safe during challenging data-based conversations in which we monitor our individual and collective effectiveness. The sample norms outlined in figure 4.2 provide examples of team commitments aimed at creating a culture of safety that can eventually serve as the basis for trust.

The agreements outlined in figure 4.2 hold the teams in a right relationship with each other and the learners they serve.

Identifying Essential Learning

Collaborative common assessments are not used for all curricula and all standards all of the time; instead, they are used on the critical components that teams identify as so necessary to learners' success that teachers would commit to work tirelessly to guarantee mastery for all of their learners.

Collective Promises to Hold Each Other Safe

- We will never sandbag a colleague—we will equally disperse the blessings and challenges among all of our classrooms, and we will view all of our learners as our team responsibility.

- We will make decisions by consensus—when the will of the group emerges, we agree to abide by it, contribute to it, and gather data to make improvements or alternations as necessary. We will never sabotage it, passively or overtly.

- We will use data rather than opinion or personal experience to frame team decisions. If we don't have existing data, we commit to gather them.

- If we need to change a team decision, we will take it to the group for review and approval.

- We commit to share strategies, practices, tools, and resources to support the success of all members of the team. We will make agreements about which materials we will use and how we will gather data regarding effectiveness of those materials.

- We will maintain confidentiality. Data are public, but what's said here remains private as we work through the complex issues and craft knowledge of teaching.

- We will never speak from the place of evaluation, positively or negatively, about our individual results. Instead, we will speak of which learning targets, which students, and which instructional strategies are required to support continued learning.

- We will speak about learners respectfully, supportively, and positively at all times—as if they are in our midst during our discussion. We will focus on their assets and capabilities as we strive to address gaps or concerns.

Figure 4.2: Sample team norms.

It is imperative that teams isolate their essential learning—sometimes called priority standards—to identify strategically when and where in the curricular units these should be taught and assessed so teams can best monitor for success. Teams do not ignore standards that are not deemed essential; ultimately, all standards are necessary. Some standards, however, are more significant than others, and as such, they will require more time and focus during instruction. Essential learnings should be large overarching standards under which many smaller standards will fit.

Many educators have expressed appreciation for the emerging standards and the accompanying, more rigorous assessments available for review. While it is true that there are fewer standards, there are still too many. At the time of the printing of this book, only mathematics and English language arts Common Core standards are completed, and already a fourth-grade teacher faces over forty-five standards *without* standards from the other content areas. And though the standards might be fewer and more tightly spiraled over time, they are also denser. The bottom line is that teachers still need to unpack and prioritize the Common Core, state, or other national standards they are tasked with delivering.

Along these lines, teachers have many questions:

- How do we begin to determine what's essential and prioritize the standards?

- Does prioritizing mean some things are completed, but others are not?

- How do we create vertical alignment in our teaching to make sure we are building on the work of previous grade levels and not reteaching everything as we have done in the past?

These questions are worthy of thoughtful responses on behalf of leaders in schools and districts. Since the early 2000s, educators have identified what was essential for students to learn by employing the three criteria outlined by Douglas Reeves (2002) to help them make their decisions.

1. **Endurance:** Will the standard provide students with knowledge and skills that will be of value beyond a single test date?

2. **Leverage:** Will the standard provide knowledge and skills that will be of value in multiple disciplines?

3. **Readiness for the next level of learning:** Will the standard provide students with the essential knowledge and skills that are necessary for success in the next grade or the next level of instruction?

Then in 2003, Ainsworth added the criterion of whether or not a standard was tested and even how much weight or value it had in the high-stakes environment.

4. **Tested:** Will the standard be tested by an accountability feature (state or national test or district benchmark)?

However, with Common Core standards, an additional question regarding testing emerges: *How* will the standard be tested? Though still in the early stages of implementation, it seems as if the Common Core and next-generation standards will do a better job of engaging learners in *using* content through meaningful processes to accomplish deep learning. The "tested" criteria for determining priority standards might better read as follows: Will this standard be tested by an accountability feature (state or national test or district benchmark), and if so, *how*? What are the cognitive demands involved?

If there is a mismatch between the content provided during classroom instruction and the cognitive complexity demanded in the tasks found in external testing, then learners will likely fail where educators most desire them to succeed (Schneider et al., 2013). For example, while the Common Core standards still incorporate grammar, testing regarding grammar will not include having students name the parts of speech or diagram sentences. Instead, Common Core testing will require students to write fluently, clearly, and accurately. Likewise, while literary devices are still listed in the core standards, having learners identify or define key terms will not test them. A student's understanding of literary devices will be tested by requiring students to engage in literary analysis as they critique whether or not a given text qualifies as quality literature. Teams will have to look at sample assessment items as they make decisions about their priority standards.

Another important criterion to consider when prioritizing standards involves student needs.

5. **Student needs:** Where are our students in their ability or understanding of this standard? Will it require sustained instructional attention, or do our students already have a relatively firm foundation with the necessary knowledge or skills in this area?

Teams must explore their various data sources for indications as to what their learners require. It is important for districtwide curriculum and assessment teams to note that learners' needs may be different from school to school. If outside assessment data indicate that learners are struggling with reading comprehension of complex text, then the standards-related complex text must become a priority feature for the teachers in that school. It is possible for one school to have a different set of priorities than another school within the same district or under the same board. This is especially so in large districts where the needs of learners can vary radically from one side of the community to the other. In the end, all learners must master all standards, no matter their initial needs. But the instructional entry points and the primary assessment focal points must be based on the needs of the learners in front of the teachers at that time if the required learning is to be meaningful to the learners.

Many different processes are available for unpacking a standard. Teams can use any process that seems easiest and most efficient for them, but it is best if that process immediately leads the team members into understanding the implications for their assessment design. Because standards are written so differently, using a single protocol doesn't always work. Within the Common Core, for example, the mathematics and ELA standards are organized in very different ways. Even if teams find a protocol that seems to work in general, they may still have to tweak the protocol to be successful with unpacking the standards. Protocols can be helpful, but ultimately teams have to make the protocol work for them and not the other way around. A protocol for unpacking standards can be found in this book's companion, *The Handbook for Collaborative Common Assessments* (Erkens, 2016).

Simply put, there will always be too much to teach without enough time to accomplish the task. Though educators openly dream of the day when they will not need to determine what's essential, they actually cannot afford to lose the option, for to do so would mean teachers had been handed a scripted curriculum with limited options for responsiveness. Decision making may be challenging, but defaulting to simple compliance is threatening. Fortunately, many experts have created protocols to support this work, and two such protocols have been provided in this book's companion, *The Handbook for Collaborative Common Assessments* (Erkens, 2016).

Developing Shared Knowledge

Once standards are prioritized, teams will need to define learning targets. Typically, this does not all happen at one time, as it would be too labor intensive for teams to prioritize and unpack their standards before school begins. In order to come to critical agreements on what's essential, teams must develop shared knowledge around the big ideas and the specific terminology within a standard. Oftentimes, developing shared knowledge involves deconstructing standards into learning targets.

Learning targets are found in standards. A learning target is the smallest, most isolated bit of information that can be extracted from a standard and assessed in isolation. The target is what teachers aim to hit with instruction, and it is what they will eventually certify was indeed mastered by each individual learner. Unfortunately, finding learning targets is not as easy as simply counting the bullet points that may be found in the standard. Sometimes a single bullet point can have multiple learning targets in it, and sometimes a single bullet point is a target all by itself. Teams must take the time to talk about their standards and targets. This simple step can help teams build coherence and clarity regarding their upcoming instructional efforts.

In the research on classroom assessment, the power of teachers naming and using learning targets in their classroom cannot be overstated. Experts agree that providing students with the targets so they know what they are supposed to learn is one of the most powerful things the teacher can do to support learning and ultimately increase achievement (Chappuis, 2009; Chappuis et al., 2012; Hattie, 2009, 2012; Moss & Brookhart, 2012; Wiliam, 2011). Learning targets are powerful for many reasons.

- **Learning targets guide instruction:** Collectively, learning targets form the scaffolding to success on the overall standard.

- **Learning targets guide assessment design and use:** Targets are assessed formatively to monitor for student mastery. Several data points demonstrating mastery over time would indicate that a learner was ready to certify mastery in a summative assessment.

- **Learning targets guide a learner's instructional decision making:** When teachers provide accurate, specific data and feedback regarding learning targets, they make transparent the vision of the target, the learner's current level of mastery with the target, and the specific, focused next steps required to help the learner attain mastery of the target.

When teachers provide feedback based on learning targets, they can promote learners' abilities to self-regulate by activating the following strategies to succeed academically.

- Engaging in self-observation (monitoring one's activities), self-judgment (evaluation of one's performance), and self-reactions (reactions to performance outcomes)

- Identifying their academic strengths and weaknesses

- Attributing their successes or failures to factors within their control (such as effort expended on a task, effective use of strategies)

- Establishing a repertoire of strategies to tackle the day-to-day challenges appropriately

- Maintaining a growth mindset

- Accepting and even seeking challenging tasks, and then rehearsing and refining knowledge and skills to develop a deep understanding of subject matter

Learning targets are central to quality instruction and assessment practices. When teachers lead by referencing targets, they can empower their learners to monitor their own learning and ultimately address their own gaps in understanding.

A closer examination of the types of learning targets underscores the importance of well-defined learning targets to effective assessment design. Assessment experts from the Portland, Oregon-based Pearson Assessment Training Institute, Jan Chappuis, Rick Stiggins, Steve Chappuis, and Judy Arter (2012) outline five types of targets: (1) knowledge targets, (2) reasoning targets, (3) skill targets, (4) product targets, and (5) disposition targets; whereas Shirley Clarke (2008), an assessment expert based in Europe, suggests there are two types of targets: (1) open and (2) closed. For the purposes of developing common assessments in an efficient manner, it seems most useful to categorize learning targets as specific or strategic. This process comes in handy when teams begin developing assessment blueprints that align their individual content (specific targets) with shared skills and processes (strategic targets) across content areas.

Specific learning targets are context dependent. They can usually only be assessed during a particular unit of study or in a particular way. For example, such targets may be stated as *Explain the New Deal policies* or *Describe the economic effects of the Great Depression.* Specific learning targets are most often (but not always) measured by right or wrong answers.

Strategic learning targets are generalizable. They are not contingent on a specific context, curriculum, or isolated details because they are skills or process oriented. As such, strategic learning targets can be assessed in multiple assessment formats or experiences over time. For example, the strategic learning target, *Cite the textual evidence that most strongly supports an analysis of what the text says explicitly as well as inferences drawn from the text,* can be assessed through a variety of stories or nonfiction literature. It can be assessed over time and across multiple disciplines. Because strategic learning targets are not specific or text dependent, it is possible to have many plausible answers, so strategic learning targets require quality criteria, scales, or rubrics to score student responses for accuracy.

When teams know their specific and strategic learning targets, they can create their assessment blueprint or architectural structure:

> The construction of valid classroom measures requires planning the test along two dimensions. The first dimension is central to content validity [consider the specific learning targets], and the second is the level of cognition [consider the strategic learning targets] the test items will require. The two axes can be plotted together in a test construction blueprint known as a table of specifications. (Wright, 2008, p. 175)

Teams who use assessment blueprints experience the following benefits:

- Increased alignment to standard expectations
- Ease in designing collaborative common assessments
- Improved valid and reliable assessments
- Focused energy to support increased student achievement

By nature, assessment blueprints force the issue of careful design with classroom assessments. For this reason, the process of identifying learning targets is not exclusive to the foundation of collaborative common assessments. Teams are constantly developing shared understanding of their predetermined essential learning, so the process of unpacking standards also occurs during the common assessment planning phases. It is critical that teams revisit their essential learning expectations and clarify their learning targets within those expectations as they are designing their summative assessment and formative pathways.

Examining School Data and Establishing SMART Goals

In the absence of outside data sources, districts and schools have no way of identifying where they stand in regard to student achievement relative to where they need to be standing. Granted, the data gathered to date have not always been the most relevant, provocative, or productive when it comes to drawing helpful conclusions that guide school improvement efforts. For that reason, it is always important to examine alternative and aligned sources of information when possible to isolate anomalies, explore patterns, and validate findings. When schools and teams seek to triangulate data, they are able to make better decisions that specifically target student needs.

Collaborative common assessments are used to address known achievement gaps by bolstering student learning in strategic places. The data should help teams narrow their focus as they develop SMART goals. In the professional learning community literature (see, for example, DuFour et al., 2008), SMART stands for:

- Strategic and specific

- Measurable

- Attainable

- Results oriented

- Time bound

SMART goals provide measures of incremental success while marching toward the ultimate goal that eventually all students will learn at high levels. So, for example, the SMART goal *78 percent of all eighth-grade students will score proficient on the state mathematics test by the end of the 2014–2015 school year* cannot remain at 78 percent or drop to an even lower percentage for the 2015–2016 school year. In a PLC, the goal must eventually be to get 100 percent of the students to learn at high levels as early and as often as possible. Educators cannot expect less of their students over time.

SMART goals anchor the work of common assessments. They provide the focus for the teams' work and the measures against which the teams monitor progress over time. Once the members of a team have written their SMART goals, they must identify the target areas that require attention within the goal area (Conzemius & O'Neill, 2014). This decision is based on the data that were culled from the battery of assessments the team members explored when identifying their priority focus or standards. For example, if the teachers had discovered their learners had been struggling in mathematics, with 64 percent of the students passing the previous year's state test, they might set their SMART goal to read: *78 percent of all eighth-grade students will score proficient on the state mathematics test by the end of the 2014–2015 school year.* While the goal is currently measurable, it is far too big for teams to have success with tracking progress. As teams explore the state data, they can see the three strands that caused their students the most trouble.

- Analyzing and solving linear equations
- Problem solving involving measurement
- Interpreting and analyzing data

The targeted areas are then linked to the SMART goal in a tree diagram (modified from the work of Conzemius and O'Neill [2014]) in figure 4.3.

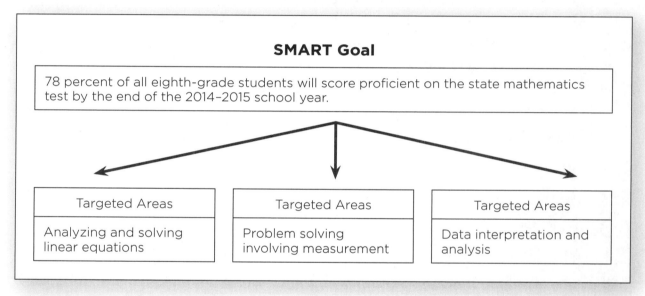

Figure 4.3: SMART goal tree diagram.

Once teams have isolated the targeted areas for monitoring over time, they can begin to identify the following for each targeted area:

- Types of assessments that will be used to monitor the target area
- The timing and placement of those assessments
- The proficiency levels required of each assessment

They may even begin to create a database of the possible instructional strategies they could consider using for each of the targeted areas. More importantly, teams could begin to document the re-engagement strategies they use for struggling learners following core instruction and then create documentation regarding the effectiveness of each strategy based on the follow-up assessment results. In this manner, teams become collective researchers of their craft knowledge.

Mapping Targets and Collaborative Common Assessments

Teams will experience more success in monitoring and supporting student learning when they are clear about the learning targets and purpose of each assessment. Creating an assessment road map provides a clear instructional pathway for teachers and their learners alike. An assessment road map can also deprivatize the instructional pathway for teachers and demystify the assessment journey for their learners. The work of collaborative common assessments is meant to support the classroom teacher. It is not meant to be a "gotcha." Just like their students, teachers must always see when the common assessments will take place and what will be on them if the teachers are to be successful.

After teams have identified their learning targets, they generate an assessment map, which will indicate where all of the learning targets will be assessed. The assessment map provides the skeleton of needed assessments. Team members are welcome to add additional assessments or modify their classroom options as long as they can verify with evidence that they have addressed the basic expectations. An assessment map highlights the bare minimum of assessments to guarantee that all learning targets are sufficiently assessed so learners can be ready for the summative assessments. Figures 4.4 and 4.5 (pages 66–67) provide examples of what an assessment plan might look like. Figure 4.4 provides an elementary example, while figure 4.5 provides a secondary example.

In the example shown in figure 4.4, the H in H1, H2, and H3, for example, indicates homework or practice. The CP, or checkpoint, provides a formal formative data point at which the student performs without outside interference. The assessment map outlined in figure 4.4 suggests learners will have to engage in two summative assessments: One is a project, and one is a final in which the learner will be given an unfamiliar passage and have to apply the strategies learned during the unit. The *X*s inside the boxes highlight which target will be assessed in each of the assessments. At this point, the team has only outlined minimum expectations for assessing the targets and has delineated where the targets will be located. The team must now determine which of those assessments will be common.

Similar to figure 4.4, figure 4.5 (page 67) illustrates an array of assessments that will be used to monitor progress: homework, close reads, quizzes, a formal paper, and an essay exam.

Common Core State Standards, Reading Informational Texts

Target 1: **RI.3.1** Ask and answer questions to demonstrate understanding of a text, referring explicitly to the text as the basis for the answers.

Target 2: Determine the main idea of a text.

Target 3: **RI.3.2** Recount the key details and explain how they support the main idea.

Target 4: **RI.3.3** Describe the relationship between a series of historical events, scientific ideas or concepts, or steps in technical procedures in a text, using language that pertains to time, sequence, and cause/effect.

Assessments: (H) homework, (CP) checkpoint, (Project) projects, and (Final) final assessments

	H1	H2	H3	CP1	H4	H5	CP2	H6	H7	Project	Final
Target 1	X	X		X					X	X	X
Target 2		X	X	X		X	X			X	X
Target 3			X		X	X	X	X	X	X	X
Target 4					X		X	X	X	X	X

Source: NGA & CCSSO, 2010a.

Figure 4.4: Elementary assessment map example.

Unlike figure 4.4, figure 4.5 highlights which specific items on the assessment will relate to the target (for example, in H1, questions 1, 4, 6, 9, and 10 will relate to target 1, while questions 2, 3, 5, 7, and 8 will relate to target 2, and so on). Some of the assessment in this map requires scoring with scales and rubrics. The team is using rubrics during the formative process to provide learners with specific, descriptive, and diagnostic feedback regarding key criteria; and the teachers are using proficiency scales with the summative features at the end of the unit so that the learners are provided with a single proficiency level against the collective whole of the standard. The team members have made sure their rubric and proficiency scale are in tight alignment so learners can readily transfer and integrate the information between the two tools without surprises or confusion.

When teams develop their assessment maps, they must decide which assessments will be formative and which will be summative before beginning the unit. Decisions made at this juncture are based on best educational estimates. It's possible that once the team members begin providing instruction, they realize some of their formative assessments may be too far above or below the intended mark. In that case, the teachers must reconvene to reconsider and redesign their assessment plan. All members of the team must participate and must be in agreement with that kind of a decision. Teams can change their original agreements as long as everyone agrees to the change in advance of providing the assessment to the learners. In other words, one teacher cannot unilaterally decide to change the plan without inviting the others into conversation and coming to agreement on next steps.

Standard: **WHST.6–8.1** Write arguments focused on discipline-specific content.

Target 1: WHST.6–8.1a Introduce claim(s) about a topic or issue, acknowledge and distinguish the claim(s) from alternate or opposing claims, and organize the reasons and evidence logically.

Target 2: WHST.6–8.1b Support claim(s) with logical reasoning and relevant, accurate data and evidence that demonstrate an understanding of the topic or text, using credible sources.

Target 3: WHST.6–8.1c Use words, phrases, and clauses to create cohesion and clarify the relationships among claim(s), counterclaims, reasons, and evidence.

Target 4: WHST.6–8.1d Establish and maintain a formal style.

Target 5: WHST.6–8.1e Provide a concluding statement or section that follows from and supports the argument presented.

Assessments: (H) homework, (CRR) close read and response, (Q) quiz, paper, and essay exam

	H1	CRR1	H2	CRR2	Q1	H3	H4	Q2	CRR3	Paper	Essay Exam
Target 1	1, 4, 6, 9, 10	Rubric	1–3					Rubric	Rubric	Scale	Scale
Target 2	2, 3, 5, 7, 8	Rubric	4–5		Rubric	Rubric			Rubric		
Target 3				Rubric			Rubric		Rubric		
Target 4				Rubric		Rubric	Rubric		Rubric		
Target 5		Rubric	6–10	Rubric		Rubric	Rubric	Rubric	Rubric		

Source: NGA & CCSSO, 2010a.

Figure 4.5: Secondary assessment map example.

An assessment map serves as a guide to help teams make strategic decisions. Imagine that in figure 4.4, the elementary team teachers have decided that checkpoint 1 and checkpoint 2 will be their common formative assessments and the project will be their common summative assessment. However, teachers will use the rest of the assessment map to guide their own classroom instruction. At a minimum, teachers will guarantee that the specific targets desired were assessed in the identified assessments on the map, but they may choose to use different questions or more prompts or activities within those assessments to do so. In addition, teachers may choose to do more homework or provide more checkpoints than the team initially agreed to do. They cannot, however, choose to do less since the team has established the baseline of what it will take to assess the standard.

The road map, then, is as much a part of the process of developing common assessments as it is a bridge between the development of SMART goals and the achievement of SMART goals. When the entire system is aligned thoroughly and in wise and productive ways, learners and teachers alike experience dramatic success.

Monitoring Progress

Once SMART goals have been written, teams use data from the common assessments to monitor their progress along the way. If teams forget this step and do not look at their data on a regular basis, they can easily miss their goal. It is akin to checking a road map in advance of venturing on a long journey but never revisiting the road map in the midst of the journey. Teams increase the probability that they will miss their mark when they do not continually compare their data against their target goals.

Collaborative Common Assessments in Action: Progress Monitoring

The leader of a fourth-grade team noticed that the team's collective scores were fluctuating radically from one assessment to the next. The only pattern of consistency was that there was no upward trajectory. She called a team meeting and began the meeting by reminding the members of their SMART goal ("85 percent of all fourth-grade students will be reading at grade level by the end of the school year") as well as their three targeted areas for growth: comprehension, fluency, and vocabulary and word attack skills. She then showed the aggregate data from the past five team common assessments in the area of comprehension: on the first of the five assessments, sixty-three percent of students passed at grade level; on the subsequent assessments, fifty-seven, seventy-two, forty-nine, and fifty-four percent of students passed at that level.

She asked the members of the team if they thought it was possible to meet their SMART goal given that they were already into the second semester of the school year. The teachers, looking somewhat befuddled, quietly shook their heads no. When she asked them why they thought their scores were so erratic or what they thought they could do about it, the team was stumped. Finally, one brave teacher asked what others thought might have led to their midpoint success of 72 percent. Someone replied, "You know what that was? That was the only time we planned the assessment together in advance of instruction." Immediately, the team members resolved to begin designing future assessments together before instructing and then looking at the results next to their SMART goal on a steady basis for the rest of the school year. At the end of the year, the team members were happy to report a steady and upward trajectory that brought them to 80 percent of their learners reading at grade level by the end of their fourth-grade year.

A Culture of Respect

Context matters. Individual teachers on teams or teams working within larger buildings will not take risks or divulge truths or openly share helpful strategies if there is perceived danger. It is imperative in the work of collaborative common assessments that educational leaders of all walks—from teacher leaders to central office administrators—attend to the larger system and culture in which they embed the work of collaborative common assessments. Decades of large-scale testing have proven that the sheer weight of constant monitoring, snap judgments, and public blame can kill hope and efficacy. Education must be about igniting curiosity, stirring passion, and kindling lifelong intrigue for learners *and* teachers. It's time then for teaching teams to name and claim their vision for their learners, to collectively engage in risk taking and exploration, and to track progress in a manner that builds hope and efficacy for all.

5

Designing Collaborative Common Assessments

Design is not just what it looks like and feels like. Design is how it works.

—Steve Jobs

Mastering the collaborative design process will build assessment literacy, establish clarity, and improve instructional agility for an entire team of teachers. Though it happens early in the process of collaborative common assessments, the design phase has just as many benefits (if not more) to offer teams as the delivery and data phases. Research summarized by James H. McMillan (2013b) regarding classroom assessment clearly indicates there is a need to develop assessment literacy for teachers: "a generalized finding was that, by and large, teachers lack expertise in the construction and interpretation of assessments they design and use to evaluate student learning" (p. 5). When teams engage in the design phase collaboratively, the rewards far outweigh the challenges involved: teams are able to clarify their shared instructional focus, prioritize curricular decisions, increase the rigor of their formative practices, and find time to accomplish what matters most for all of their learners. So much is lost when the design phase is skipped altogether and teams are handed assessments to use.

It is critical that teams complete the design process *before* starting the unit of instruction in the classroom. Teams will quickly embrace any process that paves the way for smooth instructional practice; on the other hand, they will detest and avoid any process that interrupts their instructional flow. If teams do not design their common summative assessments and their formative pathway in advance of instruction, they will constantly need to retrofit the key ideas or skills or, worse, modify past instruction to make the assessments work. At that juncture, common assessments become a despised nuisance, and teams will engage begrudgingly or quit altogether. Designing common summative assessments during instruction makes the process clumsy. Likewise, designing common summative assessments after instruction promotes curricular chaos, generates flawed results, and increases the burden now allocated to the re-engagement system.

Learners win when teachers develop their summative assessments before they begin teaching. With the common summative assessments articulated, teaching teams are better able to design a formative pathway that allows them to monitor learning along the way and even create, alter, or delete any formative assessments as needed in a responsive fashion. Time is saved, flexibility increases, and individual teachers improve their instructional power and prowess.

The Design Phase

Teams will find they have an easier time designing collaborative common assessments if they have done the context work in advance (establishing team norms for collaboration, identifying and developing shared knowledge of essential learning, examining school data and establishing SMART goals, creating a road map of collaborative assessments and targets, and monitoring progress on SMART goals). Figure 5.1 outlines the general components involved in the design phase.

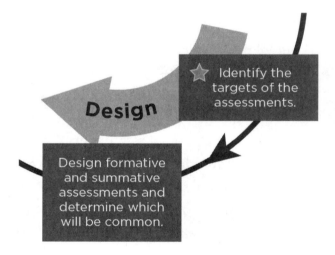

Figure 5.1: The collaborative common assessment design phase.

The star in the diagram indicates the starting point in this phase. Teams must always revisit their standards and formally unpack them if they have not already been unpacked. If the standards were unpacked earlier, then teams still engage in ensuring their targets are accurate, manageable, and put into student-friendly terms before they actually design their assessment pathways. Because common assessments should align with the expectations outlined in the team's prioritized standards, teams begin by unpacking their priority standards to find learning targets, creating and organizing a list of manageable targets for their instructional unit, and then putting the learning targets in student-friendly terms. Once the targets are identified, teams can move into the work of creating assessment maps or pathways to support instruction, making decisions regarding where the common assessments will be, designing the summative assessments with some supporting formative assessments, and then reviewing the assessments for quality.

Teams may not be ready to engage in all of the steps early on, but getting started is the most important way teams can begin to establish sound assessment practices. Simply designing a common summative assessment before beginning an instructional unit is a great way to help the team find the benefits of engaging in this process. The additional components of the design phase naturally fall into place once teams truly strive to generate valid and rigorous summative assessments that provide quality instructional information.

Protocols for Design Work

While it would seem easier to use a predeveloped assessment, whether it comes from the curricular resources or a purchased item bank, teams will miss a golden opportunity to create shared knowledge regarding the expectations. Reading and selecting a potential question does not provide the same level of deep understanding that can lead to informed instructional decision making as co-creating the questions, prompts, and measurement tools does. When teams select a predeveloped assessment and simply agree to use it, they miss an opportunity to ensure success through clarity and consistency as they individually prepare their learners for the assessment.

In the beginning, the process can be time consuming and somewhat arduous. But, as teams become more skilled and develop a natural flow to their work, the design process can move more quickly with the guidance of protocols, algorithmic agendas used to guide conversations and next steps. Four design protocols support teams' design efforts.

1. Use an existing assessment and name the targets behind each question.

2. Divide parts among team members and develop sections.

3. Proceed target by target with contributing questions on note cards.

4. Individually develop assessments, and collectively check for alignment and rigor.

There are advantages and disadvantages to each of the four design protocols. The full protocols can be found in this book's companion, *The Handbook for Collaborative Common Assessments* (Erkens, 2016).

Protocol 1

By far the easiest protocol to use, design protocol 1 involves teams reviewing, possibly modifying, and ultimately approving predeveloped assessments together. If the team is going to use a predeveloped assessment, it is important to review the assessment question by question and learning target by learning target to guarantee that the assessment the teachers have selected will match both the learning expectations and the levels of cognitive demand that they require of their students.

Collaborative Common Assessments in Action: Design Protocol 1

The third-grade team teachers decided to use the assessments that were already embedded in their curricular resources. They began by looking at their mathematics assessment. In the margin beside each question, they documented the standard it assessed. They immediately noticed that questions 6, 7, and 8 were not tied to any of their state standards. Moreover, they discovered that the remaining twelve questions addressed eight standards, so there was no way they were going to get enough of a sampling for any standards to accurately certify their learners had mastered them. The teachers could see immediately that they would need to modify the mathematics assessment for it to work.

In the language arts assessment, third-grade students were working on classification. The assessment included some nonfiction text, and below it was a two-column table that provided classifications from the text on the left-hand side of the table. On the right-hand side of the table, students were expected to write examples of things that belonged in that specific classification from the text above. Again, the team found problems with the predeveloped assessment. The first problem involved vocabulary; terms provided in the classification list did not match the text above.

The second problem on the language arts assessment was much bigger: the last row of the table left an open box on the left-hand side, and learners were to list their own classification. Nowhere in the preceding unit of instruction were learners instructed on how to identify their own classification. The team recognized immediately that the last item of the assessment may have been intended to provide an extended opportunity for learners who were already at a level of mastery. The only way the team teachers could use the last box as an extended opportunity was if they collectively agreed that learners could achieve mastery—or a level of 3 on the proficiency scale—if they answered all of the previous questions accurately, and they would only qualify for a level of 4 on the proficiency scale if they were able to answer the last question. If the team had not stopped to discuss the problem, however, learners who were unable to fill in that last box with their own classification would have been penalized in the final grade.

When a team selects design protocol 1, all of the members must review, revise, and approve the entire assessment together before launching their instruction.

Protocol 2

One of the benefits of collaborative assessment design is increasing efficiency. In protocol 2, the team divides up parts of the assessment that need to be reviewed or developed, and charges each member with taking care of a part. Like protocol 1, this protocol requires the teachers to review the entire assessment as they assemble it and approve it before launching their instruction.

Collaborative Common Assessments in Action: Design Protocol 2

The sixth-grade science team had three learning targets on an upcoming assessment regarding energy. The teachers decided to share responsibility among the four of them by divvying out the parts to be developed. Teacher A was responsible for writing five questions for learning target 1. Teacher B was responsible for writing five questions for learning target 2. Because target 3 represented the big idea of the test, it would have the most questions, so teachers C and D shared responsibility for target 3, each agreeing to write five questions.

The team members created an architectural blueprint behind their test, as shown in figure 5.2.

Target	Questions
1	1, 2, 5, 8, 9
2	3, 4, 6, 7, 11
3 (a)	10, 12, 14, 15, 19
3 (b)	13, 16, 17, 18, 20

Figure 5.2: Sixth-grade assessment blueprint.

They also made the following agreements regarding their independent work.

- Complexity would increase over time. The first two questions in each set would be written at the knowledge level, the next two questions at the application level, and the final question in each set at the integration level.

- The integration-level questions in their assessment work would require a clear scoring guide, and the teacher who wrote the question would need to develop the scoring guide.

- All questions would be subject to review, revision, and final approval by the entire team before the assessment would be officially put together.

- Team members could use existing test questions from other sources as long as the questions accurately matched the demands of the standard and the learning target involved.

After three days, the team teachers returned to the design table to lay out their individual questions, assemble the entire assessment, and review and approve the assessment and supporting measurement tools before they launched the upcoming life science unit on energy.

Protocol 3

Design protocol 3 may take a little more time initially, but there is often a greater return on the team's investment. In this protocol, teachers write the assessment together, target by target and question by question. Teachers truly develop shared knowledge and deep understanding when they actively co-create and intentionally revise their initial thinking as they work together to create and revise.

Collaborative Common Assessments in Action: Design Protocol 3

The second-grade team was concerned about the upcoming reading assessment. The teachers wanted to write their own, yet none of them felt comfortable developing quality test items. They decided to work together by creating a series of questions per target. First, they selected the passage they wanted their learners to read. Next, they identified the first learning target, inference. Each teacher had five sticky notes and was tasked with writing one question of inference per note.

When it seemed everyone was done writing his or her five questions, the team members placed their sticky notes in the center of the table. Now they had twenty-five possible questions related to inference for the passage they selected. They began sorting the questions into piles. One pile held questions that the team considered to be lower level, and the teachers decided they would use these questions to introduce the concept of inference or to use with learners who seemed to be struggling with the concept as they got started. One pile held questions the team felt would be good for the first summative assessment. Because this was the largest pile, the team split it in half and decided to use one half for the first version of the assessment and the other half for a second version of the assessment if it would be needed. The third and final pile held questions that the team believed were quite rigorous. The team decided to set these questions aside and use them for any learners who seemed to be ready for challenge or extended opportunities.

Then the team proceeded to do the same process with the remaining learning targets. In this manner, the teachers on the team created their own item bank of leveled questions. While engaged in the process, one of the team members observed that writing quality questions of inference was challenging. She felt that if writing the questions for an assessment was a time-consuming challenge, then creating quality questions to ask spontaneously during instruction was unlikely. Another colleague noted that students would have a hard time answering questions of inference on the test if they had not experienced them during instruction. At that point, the team decided it would be important to practice writing such questions on an ongoing basis.

After several weeks and much success, the teachers decided process had been so powerful for them that they should engage their learners in the same process, and they could even use it as a common assessment. So they agreed upon a passage that they would share with their learners. They gave each of their learners three sticky notes and asked them to write three different questions of inference for the passage. The learners put their names on the back of the sticky notes so that once they were collected, the teachers could see the types of questions each individual learner was able to frame. Before collecting the sticky notes, however, the teachers asked the learners to sort them into piles in the same way that they had. The teachers paid close attention to the caliber of conversation that their learners had as they critiqued the questions before them. The team discovered that when learners write quality test questions, it can be just as powerful an indication of mastery as having the learners simply answer a test question provided to them.

Protocol 4

Design protocol 4 is more challenging, and it can certainly leave more room for error. In this protocol, the team agrees to the learning targets, levels of complexity, and architectural structure of the assessment, and then each member writes his or her own assessment for classroom use. After all of the individual assessments have been developed, teachers place them on a table, and the team reviews and approves all of the assessments. If a team uses this protocol, the members will need to review and approve their items with a little more care. In addition, they will need to factor how the item was developed as a potential variable for what went wrong during their error analysis when they look at the results.

Collaborative Common Assessments in Action: Design Protocol 4

The ninth-grade algebra team in a large urban high school decided that using the exact same common assessment could be problematic if students began sharing what was on the test between classes. Each of the seven teachers agreed to write his or her own assessment based on the team's agreements. The team got together at the end of the day and developed an architectural blueprint for the summative assessment of the upcoming unit.

- Determine if an ordered pair is a solution: questions 1–3.
- Solve a system of linear equations by graphing: questions 4–8.
- Solve a system of linear equations by substitution: questions 9–15.
- Solve a system of linear equations by elimination: questions 16–20.
- Solve real-world problems using a system of linear equations: questions 21–25.
- Graph a linear inequality: questions 26–30.

Teachers also agreed to try to reach the highest level of complexity that they could within a single target area and to write a common scoring guide for the various parts of the test.

The team members knew that they would have to monitor the quality of their various questions based on student responses, and modifications might be necessary. They agreed that they would not hold a question that turned out to be poorly written against their learners.

When all was said and done, the team members felt like they had seven quality assessments that could be used for retesting if needed. They developed a test bank instead of an item bank.

A common assessment does not have to mean the exact same test, but it *does* mean the exact same targets at the exact same level of rigor with the exact same criteria for scoring. If the team is going to use a common assessment in the form of a traditional exam that does not share the exact same questions, then certain criteria must be met.

- Teams *must* clearly identify the learning targets for the assessment.

  - If the assessment will be formative in nature, then the fewer the targets, the better the opportunity to intervene and respond accordingly.

  - If the assessment will be a unit assessment that is summative in nature and there is a strong possibility that there will need to be targeted instruction or enrichment work for the unit, then the team should limit the number of learning targets to a manageable number. Of course, there is no hard-and-fast rule, and teams must use discretion regarding what is logical regarding the content. But if a single assessment exceeds approximately five to eight targets, it becomes a lengthy and disheartening experience. Each target requires enough of a sampling to ensure understanding (generally five to ten questions per target area). The sampling for student understanding of a learning target can come from multiple assessments over time, in which case a test might have fewer questions because additional evidence has been gathered elsewhere, but that would require that teams have set up their record-keeping materials by learning target so the data can be tracked from target to target.

- Teams must collaboratively agree upon the appropriate assessment method to match the learning targets and overall standard expectations and then determine if supporting materials (checklists, rubrics, and so on) will need to be developed to accommodate the assessment.

- Teams must identify their criteria or framework for cognitive complexity so that they review questions with a consistent lens for quality. There are many different options for frameworks outlining cognitive complexity. See, for example, Marzano's Taxonomy of Objectives (Marzano & Kendall, 2007), Webb's Depth of Knowledge (Webb, 2002), Bloom's Revised Taxonomy (Anderson & Krathwohl, 2001), or Newmann's criteria for Authentic Intellectual Work (Newmann, King, & Carmichael, 2007).

- Teams must identify or develop their protocol for assessment review and acceptance. There should be no surprises at the conclusion of the collaborative work.

With these criteria in mind, let's look at the ways teams can design meaningful assessments.

Education experts and even teachers themselves express concern that teams will not be able to develop valid and reliable assessments. Yet, teachers are engaged in the process of developing and employing classroom assessments on a daily basis. The best way to tackle the issue is to engage teams in thoughtful design and revision activities. According to author Robert Wright (2008), "All teachers can build valid and reliable classroom measurements" (p. 174). Teams need time and the right tools to engage in critical review of their assessment designs. The tools, like standards, assessment maps, curriculum maps, test blueprints, frameworks for calibrating rigor, and assessment review protocols, are neither challenging to find nor complex to use.

Design Considerations

The collaborative common assessments that schools need must be focused on the significant processes and 21st century skills that learners will need tomorrow. The dominance of selected-response assessments (because they are considered more efficient and cost-effective to use and more generative of fast and objective data) cannot continue. Teams will need to engage in the work of developing constructed response and performance assessment options that allow learners to experience deeper learning opportunities and high-quality assessment. The following guiding principles can help teams design the accurate and efficient assessments needed in classrooms.

- Focus on assessing concepts and skills worth mastering.

- Deconstruct the standards to identify the specific and strategic learning targets and then align assessment questions, prompts, tasks, and scoring tools *tightly* to the exact targets.

- Demystify tasks, criteria, and standards throughout instructional activities to encourage thorough preparation.

- Simulate real challenges facing people in a field of study or life beyond the classroom walls, emphasizing questions requiring thought and knowledge.

- Allow for ill-structured challenges (messy problems with many plausible solutions and unpredictable outcomes) when possible.

- Allow for assessment tasks and prompts to match student learning styles and interests.

- Minimize bias to the degree possible. Note that barriers to generating accurate results can come from a variety of sources—the test, the learner, the one scoring.

- Review and approve assessments in advance of instruction.

Many great resources are available to help teams understand how to design accurate assessments. While learning from experience helps, it is likely not sufficient when it comes to filling the gaps in assessment literacy. Districts or individual schools can best serve their learning teams by providing professional development, resources, and tools that help teams design quality assessments.

Collaborative Common Assessment Methods

All three of the formal assessment methods—selected response, constructive response, and performance assessments—can and should be used for the collaborative common assessment process. The most popular version of a common assessment involves the traditional selected-response test format, often because it replicates high-stakes testing and because it is efficient for scoring purposes. Teachers get fast data from what might be perceived to be the most objective testing format because there are definitive right answers. However, when it comes to designing and using assessments, what's fast and easy isn't always what's best. If the assessment method does not match the demands of the standard, then the entire assessment provides an inaccurate representation of mastery. Moreover, all assessment methods have the potential for bias, even when there are clear right answers involved.

The new national emerging assessments include selected-response, constructed-response (short and extended), and performance assessment methods. Whatever the subject matter, the new selected-response items strive to increase rigor by engaging learners in strategic and specific standards, the integration of multiple skills or concepts, and isolating plausible misunderstandings or missteps. The short constructed-response items—provided in both mathematics and ELA areas—require students to show succinctly their ability to comprehend and apply concepts and sometimes multiple skills or multiple steps in real-world applications. Extended constructed-response items require learners to demonstrate their command of the content and their skills by involving them in either multiple-step problems or multiple texts. The work the learners are asked to produce involves generating responses to complex problems or framing arguments or insights that lead to plausible solutions. Table 5.1 provides an overview of the various methods of assessment and their appropriate fit with the collaborative common assessment process.

As table 5.1 illustrates, there is no single assessment method that can be used for all purposes. The data generated from such methods vary greatly, and each method has its own barriers to being efficient or accurate as a common assessment.

Table 5.1: Collaborative Common Assessment Methods

Method and Descriptor	Target Alignment	Advantages as a Common Assessment	Disadvantages as a Common Assessment
Selected Response Selected-response assessments are best recognized as the typical pencil-and-paper test. Students provide right or best answers to a variety of questioning formats that may include any or all of the following— • True or false • Multiple choice • Matching • Fill in the blank • Label the diagram	**Specific Targets** Strong match **Strategic Targets** Acceptable match *if* the questions are framed to elicit reasoning or skill	• Scoring and resulting data can be digitized. • The structure is familiar and will be replicated in external assessments. • Data analysis including item analysis can be provided immediately.	• Students may know more than they were asked, but they can only answer the questions they were asked. • There is potential for bias with second language learners or struggling readers. • The method falls short of meeting the demands of 21st century skills. • Guesswork and cheating can skew results.
Constructed Response Constructed-response assessments include open-ended questions or prompts that require learners to write out or construct their answers. Constructed-response items are scored with rubrics, proficiency scales, or scoring guides.	**Specific Targets** Strong match **Strategic Targets** Strong match	• Students can explain all that they know and understand. • Reasoning can be easy to evaluate. • Misconceptions can quickly be exposed. • Teachers can integrate learning targets in meaningful ways.	• Writing a quality prompt is challenging. • Generating common data is hard; it requires inter-rater reliability. • There is high potential for bias and subjectivity in scoring. • It is time-consuming for students to prepare and for teachers to score. • It is challenging for struggling readers, writers, and second language learners.

Method and Descriptor	Target Alignment	Advantages as a Common Assessment	Disadvantages as a Common Assessment
Performance Assessment A performance assessment is an assessment that requires the assessed to either perform in front of an audience or produce a product. Performance assessments must be scored based on predetermined criteria for quality and performance levels outlining proficiency.	**Specific Targets** Acceptable match if the performance involves providing content knowledge, but in many performances knowledge is assumed **Strategic Targets** Strong match	• Students can explain all that they know and understand. • Reasoning can be easy to evaluate. • Misconceptions can quickly be exposed. • Teachers can integrate learning targets in meaningful ways. • Oftentimes there may be immediate feedback from a broader audience.	• Writing a quality prompt or series of tasks is challenging. • Many formatives may be required to support readiness. • Generating common data is hard; it requires inter-rater reliability. • There is high potential for bias and subjectivity in scoring. • It is time-consuming for students to prepare and for teachers to score. • It is challenging for struggling readers, writers, and second language learners.
Personal Communication	**Specific Targets** Strong match **Strategic Targets** Strong match	This method is not an acceptable match for common assessments.	

Personal communication is a powerful instructional assessment tool, and master teachers rely heavily on it to support their instructional decision making. However, it is not a quality common assessment model. If personal communication occurs in a common assessment setting, it would require criteria for consistent scoring for data-gathering purposes, which immediately moves the assessment into the performance arena. It has been argued that asking learners to simply share how they are feeling about the learning at hand can be a quality common assessment (for example, 72 percent of our learners are feeling confident, 21 percent are unsure, and 7 percent are feeling lost in their understanding). While such data might be nice to know, and should certainly alter how teachers address their learners directly, the data are unreliable for planning targeted re-engagement strategies. It is entirely possible for self-reported data to be inaccurate because of belief systems, preconceived notions, flawed interpretations, and so on. If teachers respond to such data with targeted strategies, they may be wasting precious time.

Toward a Deeper Understanding of Assessment Literacy

Since the 1980s, when large-scale assessment systems gained momentum and became a driving force behind the educational system, educators have not had to attend to their own assessment literacy. The knowledge, skills, and ownership required to develop assessment literacy were easily and eagerly traded away to textbook and testing companies that ensured alignment and comprehensiveness in their research-based curricula, as well as accuracy and reliability in their measurement tools. Yet, teachers are assessing daily in their classrooms. It is time to close the gap on assessment literacy and engage teachers in deeply understanding what they are trying to assess and how best to assess it. The quality of an assessment design can only be determined from the inferences that will or will not be generated in regard to the results. The critical analysis needed to ensure accurate inferences are drawn requires multiple eyes to examine the results and multiple perspectives to unpack learning regarding future designs. Vetting assessments for quality in this regard is covered in *The Handbook for Collaborative Common Assessments* (Erkens, 2016). Designing—as opposed to simply *using*—collaborative common assessments provides a job-embedded professional learning opportunity that cannot and should not be missed in schools. Collective accuracy is vital to a team's success.

6

Delivering New Approaches to Assessment

For teachers to be able to develop new approaches to formative assessment and relate them to different theories of learning, they must be able to investigate and reflect upon their own classroom practices— particularly the way they question and give feedback to students.

—Harry Torrance and John Pryor

The use of collaborative common formative assessments happens throughout the instructional process. When teams use small and frequent formative assessments, they can problem solve challenges along the way and reduce the number of students requiring re-engaged learning on the post-side of the summative assessment. During the formative phases of the journey, teams have entered their classrooms to launch instruction based on the diligent preplanning work they have done. In figure 6.1 (page 86), the smaller iterative cycle represents teachers responding directly to what is happening in their classroom.

The delivery phase of the common assessment process requires teachers to use formative assessments, some that they preplanned and some that might emerge as needs during the instructional phases. Much of what happens at the classroom level has to do with personal communication through productive, fluid classroom discussion. Instructional changes should be based in the evidence of what is and is not working, and adjusted rapidly to support continued learning.

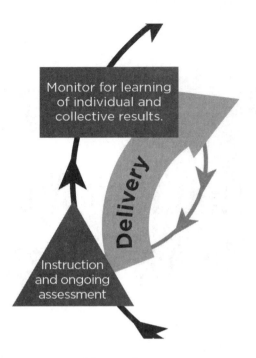

Figure 6.1: The collaborative common assessment delivery phase.

The next step, monitoring individual and collective results for learning, highlights the battery of assessments (student responses to questions, homework, bell ringer activities, exit slips, quizzes, and so on) the teacher will draw on to ensure learning is happening through the instructional process. The smaller iterative cycle sits at the heart of the formative process, and teachers should be speaking with each other regularly in an attempt to analyze errors, redirect instruction, and minimize the number of students who might require re-engagement with the learning expectations following the summative assessments.

Understanding Assessments as a Way to Inform Teaching

A very common misunderstanding is that common assessments involve lockstep teaching and the loss of a teacher's creativity and instructional style. While this can happen if the greater system mandates classroom activity, it doesn't need to and truly shouldn't happen that way. Learning only happens for students when teachers are responsive to what is occurring in the moment during instruction. Sometimes this means teachers must go backward to go forward, and at other times it means they have to modify an instructional activity in the moment. If scripted teaching truly worked, then the entire process could just be digitized. In an interview with Jan Umphrey (2008), Robert Marzano states:

The art part of effective teaching is where individual teachers figure out the best ways to use specific strategies in the context of their content area, their students, and their personalities. That's art, in the sense that people have to adapt the research to their specific situations. There's no cookie-cutter approach to teaching, but good teaching does include certain things in general. (p. 16)

Collaborative common assessments provide the vehicle for teachers to better understand collectively and individually those "certain things in general." Together, they must unpack what strategies make a positive difference for their learners, including engineering engaging classroom discussions, creating rigorous questions, responding to right and wrong answers in a manner that compels further learning, and generating quality descriptive feedback. Teachers must be learners too. They deserve the opportunity to learn in a formative, safe context.

Collaborative Common Assessments in Action: Teachers Learn in a Formative Context

When the members of a third-grade team were exploring their reading data, they discovered that one of their colleagues had better results in the strand of inference. When they asked her how she got those results, she innocently replied, "I don't know. I think I just did whatever you guys did." Her colleagues responded, "Clearly you did not. Please take us through it; what's the first thing you did on Monday?"

"I began by asking all of my learners to stand around my desk and try to make decisions about who I was as a person based on the things they saw on my desk. They said things like 'We think your family is important to you,' so I would ask, 'How do you know that?' Then they identified the things they saw like my picture with my husband and my picture with my family and the pictures that my kids had made for me that were taped behind my desk. I kept asking questions like, 'What else do you notice?'

"I knew that when kids struggle to infer, they make specific kinds of mistakes, like sometimes they make wild guesses and sometimes they are very literal. So when I was asking my questions, I tried to pull out specific examples. After we had been looking at clues for a while, I asked them if they thought we always had to have clues to make a good guess. When they said they didn't know, I asked them if they thought blue was my favorite color. They couldn't find any blue on my desk, and they could see I wasn't wearing anything blue, so I asked again if they thought they needed clues to make a good guess, and this time they answered *yes*.

"When I asked them if they thought I like to read, they said, 'Yes, because there's a poster behind your desk that says *I love to read*.' After we discussed how some statements might not be true or cannot be backed with evidence, I asked them to see if there was any evidence on my desk to prove that I love to read. They of course saw books all over the place, and someone noted that I carry a book bag back and forth from work every day. One student wisely said, 'Well, we didn't ask you if you're reading them at home. We just know that you carry books every day.'

"After our Q&A, I asked them what we were doing at that time. They were excited when they said, 'We're being like CSI agents!' Then I'm into sharing the learning target with them. 'That's right! Good readers are CSI agents. They look for clues and then make good guesses. It's called *inference*. Inference is when you can make a good guess and you support it with clues from the text and clues from your background knowledge. Let's try it.'

"The kids returned to their desks. I put them into small groups, and I gave them all the same passage. We read it aloud together, and then I gave them a question of inference. They answered together as a small group. Then I asked the groups to swap papers. They had to read each other's answers and then go back up into the text with a highlighter to highlight any clues they could find that supported the guess on their page. If they didn't have enough clues, they gave the paper back to the original team and offered some helpful ideas about what other clues might help that team make a better guess. We read some of those guesses aloud and shared our thoughts about what makes a good answer to a question of inference.

"Finally, I asked them to practice in the same way but with a new text and on their own."

"Oh," her colleagues said. "You taught the concept of inference outside of the context of reading, and then re-embedded it in reading. We can do that, and we don't even have to do it the same way!"

Team members left that data meeting with renewed energy and new ideas for helping their learners better understand the challenging concept of inference before the summative assessment would occur at the end of the unit.

As the vignette shows, collaborative common formative assessments can be powerful if they offer teachers and their learners information regarding next steps. Formative assessment *is* instruction. If teachers are not using formative assessment during instruction, then they are simply covering content and hoping things stick along the way. Instruction only worked if *learning* resulted. When teams work together and engage in collaborative common formative assessments, they can generate meaningful data for targeted decision making to guarantee learning happens. If the system is managed well, fewer and fewer learners require re-engagement on the other side of a summative assessment.

(Re)defining Assessment

Contrary to popular belief, *assessment* and *evaluation* are not synonymous. The process of assessment involves employing valid tools as well as all of the activities that surround the use of the tools (design, delivery, data analysis, and responses). The Latin term for assessment—*assire*—literally means *to walk beside*. Assessment must be something teachers do with and for learners—not *to* learners.

In its purest form, assessment is the gathering of clean data with which to make an informed decision. Evaluation involves placing value on those data. In most classrooms, anything that is assessed is immediately evaluated, resulting in a mark, a score, a statement of value (such as "Excellent work!"), a sticker, or a grade that is recorded. If assessment involved the gathering of clean data, then a clean return of data would involve just the facts (or nonjudgmental data) offered in a manner that would promote continued growth with a clearly illuminated pathway to progress forward. For example, the learner might discover that he or she has mastered three of the five target areas; with these data, the learner could focus his or her own instructional plans to address the gap. He or she could set goals to master the remaining two targets, make instructional decisions on what practice or extended learning opportunities might be needed to support specific and continued learning, and then track his or her progress over time with charts or graphs. In addition, the teacher might provide descriptive, nonevaluative feedback for the learner that highlights the types of errors the learner made with each of the remaining target areas, and sends the learner in the right direction to continue his or her learning. Unless teachers are using a grading system that avoids averaging and seeks to place more value on later scores, there can be no room for premature scores that factor into final grades and ultimately sully an accurate report on whether or not the learner has mastered the content by the end of the course.

The work of collaborative common assessments must be based on the firm classroom assessment foundation. For the various common assessment delivery systems to work, classroom teachers must individually employ a balanced classroom assessment system. Traditional classroom assessment practices can fall short of truly supporting and accurately reporting learning. Many of the current assessment systems and practices in classrooms across North America need to be re-examined and redesigned.

Summative Assessment

Summative assessment involves using tools and processes after instruction to summarize and verify how much the individual learners have mastered at that moment in time. Summative assessments are imperative to the learning process. Without the summative to certify that the learners have completed the necessary knowledge and skills, teachers will only be able to know that they were progressing along a path, but will have no real indication that the learners actually arrived at the desired destination. Summative assessments offer moment-in-time data that demonstrate the comprehensiveness of the learning expectations reassembled as a whole.

Summative assessments serve a critical role in the learning process: they certify the required learning is complete by encompassing the whole of the standard or standards being assessed (Chappuis et al., 2012). After all of the instruction, the formative assessments, the feedback, and the tracking of mastery for scaffolded components in the standard, can the learners put the whole of the standard together, on their own, and in an accurate and thorough manner? Is their learning complete?

If formative assessments are the practice, then summative assessments are the big game. The question should never be, *Do we even need to use summative assessments?* Instead, the question should always be, *What summative assessment captures the essence of our learning expectations in a manner so exciting that our learners would* want *to get there?* It is crucial that summative data reflect an accurate picture of mastery against a given set of learning standards or expectations. Because it is such challenging work, collaborative teams must work together to ensure the accuracy and comprehensiveness of their summative assessment designs and their interpretations of the resulting student work.

Formative Assessment

Formative assessment processes are used to guide instruction and help *form* students. Formative assessment is a process, not an event. Educational experts are united and firm in their message that educators must do more with formative assessment. The research is clear, consistent, and overwhelming regarding the significant impact of formative assessment on student achievement (Black, Harrison, Lee, Marshall, & Wiliam, 2004; Black & Wiliam, 1998; Chappuis, 2009; Chappuis et al., 2012; Fullan, 2004; Hattie, 2009; Marzano, 2006; Wiliam, 2011; Wiliam & Thompson, 2007).

Formative assessment is integral to quality teaching. Teaching without formative assessment equates to sluggish progress with indefinite outcomes. Formative assessment and quality instruction go hand in hand, or neither moves forward at all (Chappuis, 2009; Chappuis et al., 2012; Wiliam, 2011). Masterful teachers naturally use quality assessment practices all day long. It isn't that teachers need to add more assessments; it's that they need to understand the functions and purposes of the assessments better and then employ them with sophisticated decision making for streamlined and improved teaching.

An Integrated System

Though the definitions of summative and formative assessment are straightforward, educators continue to express confusion regarding the two processes. Several aspects of the assessment process require clarification.

- An assessment is neither formative nor summative; it is what the educator does with the results that will determine whether it was summative or formative. As Schneider, Egan, and Julian (2013) clarify, "The terms *formative classroom assessment* and *summative classroom assessment* define the teacher's intended use of information, and sometimes, describe the teacher's method of collecting information about student learning" (p. 56).

- *Both* formative and summative assessments support learning and should be used to build hope and efficacy for learners. The two processes are not at odds, and one is not inherently better than the other:

  > Just as the authors of next-generation science standards are realizing, for example, that big ideas (content) and scientific practices have to be engaged together, classroom assessment researchers and developers must realize how their pieces contribute to a larger picture. There cannot, for example, be one theory of learning and motivation for formative assessment and a different one for summative assessments. (Shepard, 2013, p. xx)

  Formative and summative assessments are interconnected.

- For formative and summative assessment to work well together, the summative assessment must be developed first; otherwise, formative assessments are simply loose pebbles on a path to nowhere. The formative pathway must create instructional information for both teacher and learners that leads learners to imminent success on the summative assessment.

- *Learning* requires a formative *culture.* As part of that culture, summative assessments must be used in a manner that enables learners to improve over time and *between* summative assessments. In other words, a learner should be able to improve in his or her ability to gather data, organize data, and draw conclusions between the gas lab, the gravity lab, the heat and cooling lab, and so on. Summative assessments should not be offered in isolation, promoting one-shot opportunities to be successful. Summative assessments should still be used in a manner that engages learners in the practice of improving over time. The new standards place heavy emphasis on core processes in all disciplines with which learners should be able to improve over time.

- Learners must be involved the entire way:

  The acid test of effective formative assessment, however, is not how well-written the strategies are, or how many good techniques are in use, but the extent to which pupils are, as a result of our work, actively engaged in thinking, learning and assessing that learning. (Clarke, 2008, p. 11)

If formative assessments are done well, then learners should walk into a summative experience with clear evidence of readiness and high levels of efficacy, making the summative assessment experience nothing more than a celebration of all that has been learned along the way.

In a true learning culture, learning is never really finished, and learners engage in multiple opportunities to prove mastery. A formative culture is required for all learners to become career and college ready. Far more than simply adding obtrusive assessment tools or events to the classroom (which formative assessment should never be), the work of creating a formative system is complex: it requires unwriting and rewriting educators' paradigms of assessment altogether. The misunderstanding of the assessments already designed and employed must be corrected if educators are to develop balanced assessment systems. As Black and Wiliam (1998) assert, assessment and learning are virtually synonymous. Only when teachers engage in focused and deliberate balanced assessment practices is instruction used to *guarantee learning*.

Delivering Common Assessments Within a Unit of Instruction

When teams own the common assessment process, they find the best ways to address their learners' needs with timely and responsive instruction. Many variations exist regarding how best to do this work within a single unit of instruction. There is no algorithm for assessment use (for example, just use three formative assessments before every summative assessment in a unit, or just use four common formative assessments in the course of the year), and educators should avoid trying to create one. A successful pattern for assessment use in one unit of study will not necessarily work in the next unit of study. What must happen in the classroom with the assessment process is always going to be different based on discipline, content complexity, student readiness, the schedule of school festivities beyond the classroom walls, and a host of other variables. Some popular variations of how teams have engaged in the common assessment delivery process are provided. Unless stated otherwise, all examples are within a single unit of study.

Pretests and Post-Tests

In figure 6.2, collaborative common assessments are offered in a pretest and post-test system. In this scenario, teams give a common, formative quiz at the beginning of the unit and provide differentiated learning options throughout the unit based on the results. They work to make sure that all learners will be successful by the time they reach the summative common assessment at the end of the unit.

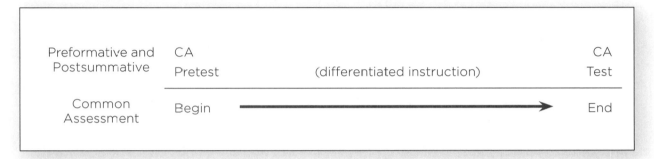

Figure 6.2: Collaborative common assessments in a pretesting and post-testing system.

Preassessments are often misunderstood and misused. According to authors Jessica Hockett and Kristina Doubet (2013/2014), "Preassessment has a bad reputation. That's largely because preassessment is so often used only to compare pre- and post-unit results, thus serving as little more than a thief of instructional time and a discouraging exercise for students" (p. 50). At their very worst, preassessments have been used to begin labeling and sorting learners into categories prior to their opportunity to experience the instruction they would need to be successful. Such a practice creates a fixed mindset for the learners themselves *and* the teachers who serve them. Continually confirming all that learners don't know—especially prior to a fair opportunity to learn something—can be one of the fastest ways to destroy hope and motivation in the classroom.

In the model provided in figure 6.2, the pretest is not the exact same test as the post-test. Instead, the pretest is devised to capture evidence of the students' readiness at the concept level, not regarding the specifics yet to be provided during the unit of instruction. Assessment-savvy teams use collaborative pretests to pique students' curiosity regarding the upcoming unit, uncover potential connections on a classwide basis regarding background knowledge or prior experiences with the topics at hand, and confirm student readiness with prerequisite knowledge or skills. Preassessments should be an opportunity to generate interest and open a pathway to motivation for learning (Hockett & Doubet, 2013/2014).

Experts in differentiation, Carol Ann Tomlinson and Tonya Moon (2013) note:

> It is useful to remember that students are not blank slates when they enter classrooms. They bring with them the impact of an array of prior experiences in other classrooms and in their own particular lives. In order for students to grow in those classrooms, teachers must have an understanding not only of the amount of prior knowledge a student brings but also the quality of that prior knowledge. (p. 422)

When teams discover what individual learners bring to the classroom in advance of instruction, they can more readily weave the experiences and stories of their learners into providing instruction, making the learners a part of the instructional process. Done well, pretests can provide formative information that shapes the instructional pathway as well as activates the learners as instructional resources to one another (Wiliam, 2011). Tomlinson and Moon (2013) continue, "It is pointless and likely harmful to persist in *teaching* students things they have long since mastered" (p. 422).

Preassessments should not cover the entire curricular unit or standard; instead, they should be short, offering a few strategic and purposeful questions. The answers to those questions should provide teachers with the instructional data they need to begin building from the base of what the learners already know and can do. Tomlinson and Moon (2013) state that "having a clear understanding of students' prior knowledge can aid a teacher in planning instruction to fit the varying range of readiness levels, interests, approaches to learning, and cultural differences that students in a classroom are likely to have" (p. 421).

When collaborative common pretests are used, the results must be used to shape the instructional pathway for the team, or the purpose of using the assessment will have been lost. Teams meet immediately following the use of a common pretest so they can explore the results and begin aligning or tweaking the instructional pathway they had anticipated using during the early stages.

Collaborative Common Assessments in Action: Using Formative Pretests to Guide Instruction

Teachers on the seventh-grade science team were about to embark on teaching their earth and life history science unit. To begin, they examined their standard closely and then created their summative assessment. Once that was done, they decided to provide a short common pretest (different from the summative assessment) through which they could pique student curiosity and identify the common misconceptions or preconceived notions that the learners would be bringing with them into the unit. The teachers decided to ask the following questions.

- How old is the Earth? Does it look the same today as it did in the beginning? Explain your answer.

- How can scientists accurately determine the age of the Earth if there was no one here at the beginning of time to record it?

- What is the Earth made of?

- Did anything exist before dinosaurs?

  ○ If so, what?

  ○ If not, why not?

- How long have humans existed?

  ○ How do we know that to be true?

The team got together at the end of the pretest and sorted the assessments into groupings of popular misconceptions. Once the teachers had identified the most popular misconceptions, they developed instructional strategies and interesting resources (videos and websites) that would help them create enough cognitive dissonance and generate enough curiosity to help their learners break through their initial understanding of the Earth and life history to create a new and more accurate understanding of the world around them.

The team organized the lessons around the popular misconceptions, created small formative checkpoints to monitor progress, and then provided differentiated options to extend learning for those students who demonstrated early understanding. The teachers checked in with each other regularly to ensure they were successful. When it came time to give the summative assessment, the team was certain that the learners were ready, and the teachers were anxious to prove their own hypothesis to be true.

Frequent Formatives

Another delivery option involves using many small common formatives along the way as illustrated in figure 6.3 (page 96). In this scenario, teams give several common, formative quizzes (four are pictured, but it could be more or less) throughout the unit of study, usually dividing up the learning strands that will be involved in the final summatives into the individual various quizzes. They provide differentiated learning options throughout the unit based on the results so they can ensure that everyone will be successful by the summative common assessment at the end of the unit.

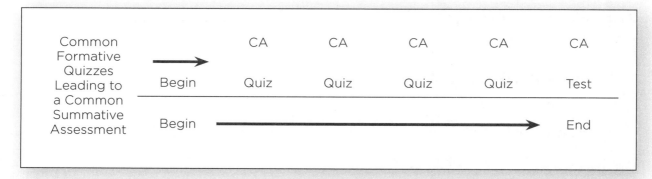

Figure 6.3: Collaborative common assessments with small quizzes for monitoring along the way.

The model outlined in figure 6.3 can provide an easy way for students to be involved as they track their progress between assessments so they can be certain to meet their learning needs by the time they arrive at the summative assessment. Teachers and learners alike should enter into the summative assessment eager to confirm and celebrate all that they have already learned. There should be no surprises at that point.

Common formative assessments do not need to be intrusive, extensive, formal, or unrelated assessment work. Rather than interrupt instruction, they should *support* it. The small checkpoints that teams might choose to use as common formative assessments should be brief and informative. Instead of quizzes, a team might consider using one of the daily bell-ringers, or opening assessment prompts for warm ups, in the course of their week, or they might create a weekly exit slip that contains one to three questions based on the work of that week's learning. Still another possibility involves selecting a question or two from the previous day's practice work and offering it again but in a quiz-like setting. When using assessment data to gather evidence of a student's current understanding or readiness, it's important that the learner provide that evidence within the purview of the instructor. If homework was done beyond the classroom walls, the instructor has no way of knowing how much additional support the learner received while doing the homework or, for that matter, who actually completed the homework. If the team chooses to use a question or two from the previous day's work, then the team will want to ask the learner to answer the questions or complete the task again, this time without additional resources around him or her.

When common formative assessments are brief, teams can analyze and respond to the data more quickly. Teams that find the resulting instructional data to be invaluable have found ways to hold expedient but thorough data meetings. If the team members decided to add a quick common formative assessment to explore or further define a phenomenon they thought their learners were encountering, they might call a flash meeting.

Flash meetings are unplanned and very brief. In a flash meeting, the team knows exactly what needs to be explored, members have generated the evidence quickly to explore it, and they use a sorting protocol to examine the evidence and make decisions. Some teams use a standing meeting. Standing meetings are either called *standing* because they happen at a consistent time (for example, the last fifteen minutes of every Wednesday) or because they are so brief that no one is allowed to sit down until the meeting is over. No matter the interpretation of *standing*, the meetings are used to quickly diagnose a limited sampling of student work (such as a single question or so), identify errors, and strategize immediate next steps.

Because common formative assessments are more about gathering evidence for instructional decision making, the learners can take them anonymously, and the teachers don't need to record the data in the gradebook. A team can generate helpful instructional information by simply using an exit slip—an index card on which learners answer a single question. They might discover, for example, that 86 percent of their learners mastered the week's expectations; of the remaining 14 percent, there were three types of errors that emerged in the students' misunderstandings. Based on those specific errors, teams can immediately plan an instructional intervention to address each area of concern prior to the summative assessment. As an added benefit to anonymous cards, classroom teachers can swap sets of cards after they have collectively agreed on what to look for in the cards and then return to their classroom for their own learners to use another class's set of cards as they explore the types of misunderstandings that might happen with the key concept they have been learning.

Teams that use models rich with common formative assessments embedded in an ongoing manner will generally state that they feel stronger in their individual classroom decision making, they know each of their learner's needs more clearly, and they find their team meetings to be synergistic and enlightening. These teams *make* time to be together because the work at the team level makes their life at the classroom level so much easier.

Collaborative Common Assessments in Action: Frequent Formatives

Teachers on the high school algebra 1 team knew they needed to do something to radically improve student performance, and they felt challenged by the demands of the new algebra 1 standards. Though they had been using common summative assessments all along, they did not feel like it was helping their learners or themselves improve. They decided to try using smaller common formative assessments during the unit on reasoning with equations and inequalities. They also wanted to engage their students in self-monitoring their progress.

They began by unpacking the standard, creating a manageable number of student-friendly learning targets, and designing the unit's common summative assessment. With that structure in place, they were then able to create a student tracking form that each algebra 1 student would use throughout the unit to monitor growth over time, target by target. The tracking form would include monitoring evidence from homework checks, quizzes, exit slips, and in-class feedback. Once the tracking sheets were completed, the team identified a learning focus for each week of the unit. At that point, the teachers were able to create exit slips for each week. The slips contained anywhere from one to three mathematics questions that focused on the learning of the week.

Once the team's teachers launched the unit, they were diligent about monitoring their progress over time by using the exit slips to check student understanding as well as to make informed instructional choices. The team gathered at the end of every Friday to review the exit slips. Teachers traded classroom sets of slips so that no one was looking at his or her own results. They quickly sorted all of the slips into piles—those that were all right and those that contained errors. From there, they divvied up the error pile and began sorting it based on the types of errors made within each slip. Once the error piles were formed, the teachers named the types of errors they found and then created instructional strategies to address the errors.

Halfway through the process, the team members decided the work was so meaningful for them that it might be beneficial for their learners as well. They began withdrawing samples from each of the error categories that did not come from their own classrooms. They removed student names, returned to their classrooms with the samples, and engaged their learners in sorting exit slips into piles based on types of errors, naming the errors, and then identifying the mathematical fix to each error.

The teachers on this team not only observed a significant increase in student accuracy and understanding but also realized they could close the gap in understanding within ten minutes if they first understood the specific type of error that had been made. As they approached the common summative assessment, they felt success was imminent. They had evidence from their small formative exit slips, the results of their reassessing after the interventions, and the student data tracking sheets to prove that learners were entering into the testing phase more prepared than they ever had been in the past.

Integrated Interventions

Some teams opt out or are unable to use many small common formative assessments during the instructional unit. Figure 6.4 outlines a model in which teams weave time to manage the intervention process near the end of their unit of instruction by extending the time frame for the summative process to be several days in length. In this model, teams give a common assessment and then engage in reteaching, coaching, or enrichments for a space of time before reassessing. The intervention window of time could be anywhere from a single day to a few hours to a full week before the unit officially ends. Once they have the data from the first assessment, they collaborate on intervention strategies and group students according to need for time allotments before the common reassessment. In this scenario, students are sometimes moved around to work with different teachers and peers, but that approach is not required and can sometimes be less than desirable, especially with very young students. When teachers have solid plans, differentiation can happen within a single classroom.

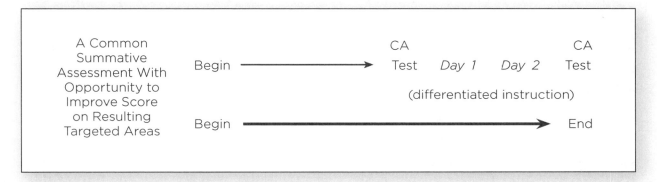

Figure 6.4: Collaborative common assessment with intervention built in.

Teams that engage in this model create unit assessment plans and curriculum mapping guides that build time for interventions into the unit design. When teams use a retesting model, popularly known as second-chance testing, it is important to note that the second test—or any of the following variations—cannot be exactly the same as the first test, especially when the first and last assessments are so close together. Rather, the assessment needs to cover the exact same targets, at the exact same level of rigor, with the same score expectations, but with different questions, prompts, or tasks. The system is meant to be one of support, so it should not penalize learners who were unable to master it the first time. In addition, learners should be tasked with retaking the entire section that applies to the missed target and not substitute questions for single items within that section. Learners should not be asked to redo the entire assessment if they demonstrated mastery in any of the other learning targets assessed.

For teams that use this model, it is also important to note that interventions must be targeted based on specific learner needs, and that reteaching must be involved. Interventions cannot include louder, slower versions of the initial instruction, and they cannot be self-managed through study guides or "packet" learning. Both learners and their teachers must invest in the journey to mastery. Teachers must set the context so that the learners understand the work is more about achieving mastery than compliance, and that being masterful in the skills involved will set them up for success. If learners are simply engaging in reassessment processes to pass a test or earn a grade, then the interventions quickly fall into activities of compliance, and many learners will be uninterested and unmotivated.

Collaborative Common Assessments in Action: Integrated Interventions

The team of second-grade teachers realized early that their second graders would need additional instruction and practice with inferring, making connections, and using textual evidence to support their work when reading. They began by identifying student-friendly learning targets in each of the three areas and then created student-friendly rubrics that the second graders would use to evaluate quality and monitor their progress. Next, they created a summative assessment for the upcoming unit, student-friendly tracking forms, a list of the stories they would use during the unit, and even an enrichment activity for their successful learners. When they introduced the targets and the rubrics, they decided to tell all of the second graders about the enrichment opportunity that would occur at the end of the unit if the learners mastered their learning expectations along the way. The second-grade students expressed great enthusiasm about the possibility of collaborating with their friends to create a storyboard that would require their teachers to infer and make connections. They loved the idea of possibly stumping their teachers, but they were most excited about storyboarding—especially if they were able to use digital tools to illustrate their stories.

Once the groundwork was set, the team teachers used stories and created a series of possible responses so that their learners could constantly engage in using the rubrics to score quality with consistency. They also engaged the learners in peer and self-scoring once the students understood the rubrics and the ground rules for being kind to each other were clearly established.

Though the teachers did not provide small common formative assessments along the way, they used team meetings to discuss the progress (or, in some cases, the lack of progress) they believed they were making as they explored student consistency with scoring.

Following their summative assessment for that unit, a large percentage required additional support with inferring, so the team decided not to conduct a major intervention with that skill; instead, the teachers immediately planned to roll continued opportunities to practice that skill into several of their future literature units. Out of ninety-three students, they still had six learners who were struggling with making connections from text to self, seventeen who were struggling with making connections from text to the world, and twenty-five learners who were struggling to make connections from text to text. Five of their learners struggled in all three categories. The team pored over the artifacts of student work and isolated the most common mistakes per category. The teachers also identified what each individual learner needed. At that point, the teachers created a series of mini lessons, coaching questions, a differentiated game plan that they would each use in their own classrooms, and another version of the summative assessment to give in three days' time.

Action Research

Collaborative common assessments can also be used as an action research tool to explore phenomena, address the needs of a specific group of learners, or generate a set of solutions to a complex problem. In figure 6.5, teams isolate both a phenomenon and a target group, then identify a potential strategy or strategies to use, and engage in the work of common assessments to monitor the success of their applied strategies. The image shows daily assessments, but the number of common assessments used would need to be a team decision based on the demands of the phenomena of study.

Common assessment as an action research tool	A weekly routine with a select group of students for a limited period of time				
	FA	FA	FA	FA	CFA
	Mon	Tues	Wed	Thurs	Fri
	(Students monitor and record data)				(Teacher records)
	Begin ⟶ End				

Figure 6.5: Collaborative common assessments as an action research strategy.

When teams use the common assessment process as an action research tool, they start by identifying a targeted need within their classrooms as well as the learners most needing support regarding that need (such as the eight readers in each classroom most struggling with fluency in reading). A team-determined set amount of time each day (for example, ten minutes) is set aside for instruction with an included formative assessment (scored not by the teacher but by students). Students are grouped as needed and track their progress daily. Teachers offer a common assessment for each student in the group at the end of each week of instruction. The team monitors data weekly, and it plans instructional responses accordingly for the following week.

Collaborative Common Assessments in Action: Action Research

Teachers on the fifth-grade team at an elementary school noticed a three-year steady decline in their state mathematics scores in their African American and Hispanic male populations. They were using all of the same strategies they had used with all of their students, but nothing seemed to be working, and they were very frustrated. After a few years of faulting the learners, they committed to making themselves vulnerable and engaging in action research to see if they could address the rapidly increasing achievement gap.

They began by framing their action research question: What strategies and actions can we use to successfully reduce an equity-specific achievement gap in fifth-grade mathematics? Once the question was framed, the team decided to take the following steps as a precursor to identifying the curriculum-, instruction-, assessment-, and classroom management-based strategies and actions they would need to use to answer their question.

- Each teacher would identify five of his or her most struggling African American or Hispanic male mathematics students to participate (the learners would know they were participating as scientists to help solve a complex problem).

- The team would write a short, six-question survey seeking feedback from the learners regarding their teacher's instruction, and the teachers would ask each of their participating learners to answer the questions within a week's time so they could begin the work right away.

- The team members gathered to sort and classify the resulting qualitative statements from the survey to see if they could find any patterns that emerged.

Initially, the team teachers were shocked to learn that the participants from each of their classrooms did not feel safe or welcome, especially during mathematics class. They felt intimidated and afraid to ask or answer questions publicly. They could not keep track of what was happening instructionally. They wanted (and needed) more time to talk about what they were learning before they were asked to practice the concepts individually.

With state results, existing classroom assessment data, and their qualitative findings in hand, the team members were now ready to identify their specific strategies and actions to reduce their achievement gap.

- For each pattern that emerged, the team created curriculum, instruction, assessment, and even a few classroom management-based solutions. The teachers agreed they would *not* modify the assessments in a manner that reduced the expected rigor, lower the standards, or set the learners apart instructionally in the classroom in any manner that would make them look different to their peers. They were going to need to find small grouping activities for all of the learners so that quick conversations with their participants would not be noticeable to others.

- They also agreed they would invite the learners into helping them evaluate the quality of those solutions while they were working with the learners.

- For each solution that emerged, they would use small common formative assessments (bell ringers or exit slips with one to three mathematics questions) to monitor the results. Again, they would invite feedback from the learners to help determine what was working and what was not socially and emotionally.

- They provided each learner with self-tracking sheets so the learners would have the tools needed to participate in gathering data and making informed decisions.

- They created their own tracking forms that highlighted their identified solutions (their targeted areas for growth) and then used both qualitative (feedback) and quantitative (common assessment scores) to explore the answer to their key question.

The team of teachers *and* their participating mathematics scientists spent the entire year making sure everyone was improving. Sure enough, the learners were closing achievement gaps, and the teachers were addressing the equity gaps that emerged in their initial findings.

Many different delivery systems are available for collaborative common assessments. Each system integrates the work of formative and summative assessments at the classroom level. When teams engage in this work the right way, they strengthen the core of their instruction.

Examining Data to Improve Learning

Exploration is the engine that drives innovation.

—Edith Widder

If collaborative common assessments are not improving the core of instruction, then they are not working. Assessment must be a diagnostic process that provides teacher and learner alike with clear next steps. In many teams, data-based conversations are stilted formalities in which learners are sorted into groups based on their test results for other experts, such as intervention specialists or gifted and talented specialists, to teach, support, or ultimately fix. The findings of such data meetings are relevant to fixing others, but irrelevant to fixing *self*. When teams sidestep the opportunity to strengthen the core of their individual and collective knowledge and skills, the *learning* aspect of professional learning community work is missed altogether. In these teams, data conversations are mechanistic, obligatory, and cumbersome.

In a true learning team, data-based conversations should include provocative inquiries, profound insights into personal and collective strengths and opportunities for growth, and creative and synergistic team-based responses that target the needs of all learners, including the needs of the teachers as learners themselves. Successful collaborative teams use data to guide their decision making and improve their individual and collective craft knowledge. Through the conversation, they find themselves learning, transforming, and even inventing. They leave data conversations rejuvenated, recommitted, and excited about the possibilities that lie ahead. They become scientists studying the impact of their own purpose-driven investigations. In such conversations, teachers are always engaged in both *being* and *becoming*.

It is rare to find data conversations that are synergistic and enlightening, to the extent that they become life giving and rejuvenating. When data conversations are stilted, it usually means one or more of the following issues are at play.

- The burden of ownership is outsourced.
- The learning that was assessed lacks heartiness.
- The conversation is not safe; data are being used to judge others.
- Ego stands in the way of acknowledging brutal truths.

Any tool can be used to create or harm. Data conversations are tools for learning that can definitely be employed in ways that obstruct learning.

The Right Kind of Data Conversations

If collaborative common assessments are the engine of collaborative learning teams, then the data are the critical fuel that keeps the engine working. Teams should be hungry for data that can provide them with the information they require to make significant decisions.

When it is time to look at the data, teams will need at least four things at the ready to support their discussion: (1) team norms to manage emotions during the crucial conversation, (2) a protocol to navigate the data with speed, focus, and accuracy, (3) the data, already aggregated and organized by teacher, by student, and by target, and (4) the students' work to look deeply into types of errors for reteaching or coaching implications. The four resources are necessary so that teachers might draw accurate conclusions regarding the results. In addition to finding successes, teams need to explore the types of simple mistakes, conceptual misunderstandings, or flawed reasoning at play for the individual. Collaborative teams are always on a hunt for quality information regarding what works so that all of their learners will be successful.

A Data Protocol

Recall that protocols are algorithmic agendas used to guide conversations. Data protocols can help keep individual members safe throughout the process while also ensuring teams remain focused on the work at hand. They offer safety in recognizable patterns, but they also offer assurance that critical steps are taken and important questions are addressed every time the team engages in data-related work. No matter the protocol they select, collaborative learning teams must always answer the following three questions during their data search and conversation.

1. **As a team:** Which targets from the assessment require more attention?

2. **As an individual teacher:** Which area was my lowest, and how can I improve in that area?

3. **As a team or individual:** Which students did not master which targets, and why?

Collectively, the answers to these questions empower teams to address the needs of individual learners as well as the growth opportunities for individual team members. *The Handbook for Collaborative Common Assessments* (Erkens, 2016) provides a data protocol to support the team's data discussions.

When teams engage in data analysis, they clarify the needs of their learners and make decisions about their individual and collective next steps. They look at the data target by target, learner by learner, and, finally, error by error. Teams might use a document similar to figure 7.1 to identify, track, and problem solve errors found in the assessments.

A Tool to Support Diagnosing Errors and Misunderstandings

Learning target:		Learning target:		Learning target:	
Number and names of students:		Number and names of students:		Number and names of students:	
What types of errors were made with this target? (Number of error categories? Names of error categories?)		What types of errors were made with this target? (Number of error categories? Names of error categories?)		What types of errors were made with this target? (Number of error categories? Names of error categories?)	
Error:	Instructional fix:	Error:	Instructional fix:	Error:	Instructional fix:
Error:	Instructional fix:	Error:	Instructional fix:	Error:	Instructional fix:

Source: Adapted from Vagle, 2015. Used with permission.

Figure 7.1: Diagnosing learning by target areas.

Which Targets From the Assessment Require More Attention?

It should not be assumed that reteaching is the automatic next step when some learners did not master the concepts. Instead, teachers can carry a target area forward into future units of instruction when many learners struggled with a similar target. Sometimes, learners will better understand a target with practice over time and after they encounter it in many different contexts. Many of the new standards have process-oriented standards that lend themselves beautifully to multiple opportunities for exposure and practice over the course of many units of content and instruction. In this manner, teams can ease up on time spent in their intervention blocks. The decision to avoid an intervention following an assessment is based on the target itself. Teachers can ask themselves a few key questions to make the decision to avoid an intervention at this juncture.

- Will the missed target areas be critical to the next steps in our instructional path (for example, will learners need it to move forward)?

- Are we done addressing the missed target areas instructionally (for example, is this the last opportunity for learners to certify mastery)?

- Is the missed target area crucial to the learners' overall success?

If the answer to any question is *yes*, then the team must incorporate an immediate intervention; however, if the answer is *no*, the team can move forward by addressing the target in future units of study and helping learners monitor their progress toward mastery of that target over time.

Which Targets Assessed Are Individual Teachers' Weakest Areas?

The individual facts, statistics, percentages, or other bits of information that make up data must be put together in meaningful ways to create information. When it comes to assessment processes, data are in the form of whole numbers, percentages, cut scores, proficiency levels, rubric scores, or grades. Percentages are all too often used as decision-making points. Numbers or any other representation of a value or level should never be decision-making points during the formative or intervention processes; instead, they serve *only* as windows into the spaces where deeper exploration is required before any quality decisions can be made. Once teams find data points that signal areas of concern (such as low test or rubric scores), they need to drill down to the next layer of data (such as by target, then by question or task) until they isolate the exact area of concern. They must turn to the artifacts so they can dig even further into the specific errors involved. Teams must carefully examine the specific evidence to diagnose learning needs, create meaningful feedback, and respond with targeted instructional interventions.

Collaborative common assessment data must always be aggregated in comparative ways—by classroom, by learner, by target—so that patterns and anomalies can be discovered and explored in depth. Figures 7.2 and 7.3 (page 111) illustrate data displays by classroom and target and by learner and target, respectively. At the secondary level, a single teacher may have too many students to place everybody on one chart, so teams might use multiple charts—the first, though, reveals the aggregate results for the team as outlined in figure 7.2.

When data are organized in this manner, teams can identify the following.

1. What is the greatest area of growth for the entire team?

2. What is my greatest area of growth as an individual on this team?

Assessment learning targets:

- I can locate information by using a variety of consumer and public documents.
- I can explain the purposes and characteristics of different forms of written text, such as the short story, the novel, the novella, and the essay.
- I can understand and analyze the differences in structure and propose between various categories of information materials (such as textbooks, newspapers, and instructional or technical manuals).
- I can assess the adequacy, accuracy, and appropriateness of the author's evidence to support claims and assertions, noting instances of bias and stereotyping.
- I can organize information in logical ways and effectively communicate my findings.

Assessment results:

	Teacher A	Teacher B	Teacher C	Teacher D	Teacher E	Teacher F	Totals by Target
Locate Information	89%	95%	97%	89%	88%	91%	**92%**
Explain Purpose	97%	92%	96%	98%	92%	94%	**95%**
Analyze Differences	91%	88%	86%	96%	77%	92%	**88%**
Assess Evidence	83%	92%	97%	86%	65%	72%	**83%**
Organize and Communicate	92%	98%	98%	85%	81%	89%	**91%**
Classroom Totals	**90%**	**93%**	**95%**	**91%**	**81%**	**88%**	

Figure 7.2: Common assessment data display by classroom and target.

While it is not yet possible to see which learners will require specific support, the team can clearly see that many learners would benefit from more practice with assessing evidence. One of the teachers' first decisions might include continuing the practice of assessing evidence in a future unit of instruction, rather than stopping instruction to engage in a large-scale intervention. The team members can also identify their individual areas of strength and opportunities for growth. At this point, teams need norms and protocols to make the conversation safe as they explore their own instructional practice and future instructional implications. But collectively these data only serve as an initial introduction into where to dig more deeply.

No matter the type of data, it is always wise to look past the initial number. It would be easy, for example, to have a public celebration regarding the data in figure 7.2, since no number drops below 80 percent in any of the overall total columns and rows (by target or by classroom). However, many student and teacher needs would not be met by such a snap decision. The initial data organization by target and by classroom simply points teachers to where they should look more deeply.

Which Students Did Not Master Which Targets, and Why?

With data organized by target and classroom, teams cannot discover the needs of the individual learners. Teams must also be able to answer *Which learners did not master which targets?* when mining common assessment data. Additionally, teams must consider data for each learner and by each target for each classroom as demonstrated in figure 7.3.

Immediately, new information emerges when teachers look at individual learners by target. For example, it is quickly apparent that an entire class average rate of 80 percent or better can hide the fact that there are still struggling learners within the individual classrooms. In the data, student O scored 60 percent, an insufficient passing mark. Such a mark at the top of any test would cause both the learner and the teacher to despair. Both will ultimately feel overwhelmed by the sheer magnitude of the 40 percent remaining to be mastered. This is why teams and learners should never make decisions based on a single data point or an aggregate score. Both learner and teacher are more likely to remain hopeful when they realize that learner O has mastered three of five targets, and only has two targets left to master.

Likewise, cut scores, a very common decision-making point, can be deceiving. In the previous data set, student D has an overall mark of 89 percent, but hiding inside that passing mark is an insufficient mark for student D's ability to analyze differences. Again, these data provide another window into where to dig more deeply. What is not yet understood simply by looking at the numbers is the type of errors the individual learners may have been making and their personal explanation of what went wrong. Data point everyone in the direction of where to

Classroom E Data for Information Literacy: Results by Student and Target

Student Name	Locate Information	Explain Purpose	Analyze Differences	Assess Evidence	Organize & Communicate	Number Correct	Percent Correct
A	5	4	6	5	9	29	**83%**
B	5	6	3	4	5	23	**66%**
C	6	6	5	4	9	30	**86%**
D	6	6	3	6	10	31	**89%**
E	4	5	4	6	8	27	**77%**
F	6	6	5	5	10	32	**91%**
G	6	5	5	5	9	30	**86%**
H	5	6	4	7	9	31	**89%**
I	5	4	5	3	5	22	**63%**
J	5	5	5	4	8	27	**77%**
K	5	6	4	2	8	25	**71%**
L	6	6	5	4	9	30	**86%**
M	5	5	4	5	7	26	**74%**
N	5	6	4	5	10	30	**86%**
O	5	6	6	2	2	21	**60%**
P	5	6	6	6	10	33	**94%**
Total Possible	6	6	6	7	10	35	**100%**
Averages	88%	92%	77%	65%	81%	30	**80%**

Figure 7.3: Common assessment data display by learner and by target.

continue their exploration. At this point, teams would require artifacts and student interpretations to make the best decisions regarding possible interventions. Reteaching an entire missed concept wholesale would not only be a tremendous burden on teacher schedules, energy, and time, but it would also be disrespectful to the learners if that instruction is not what is needed.

Research indicates that the data from classroom assessments are not currently driving instructional decision making at a level of specificity that is supportive of a learner's continued growth (Andrade, 2013; Heritage, 2013; Schneider et al., 2013; Wiliam, 2013). If there are target areas that will require immediate intervention to be able to move forward or to certify mastery for the learners, then teachers must identify specific learners, specific learning targets, and even specific areas of need based on the types of errors made within each target area.

Once the teams clearly identify types of errors that remain and the potential instructional fixes for those errors, they can organize learners into differentiated groupings required to support next steps. Because the work is managed target by target, learner by learner, and error by error, the instructional response plans naturally engage teachers in flexible grouping rather than the traditional ability grouping that can happen with categorical responses based on overall cut scores. As teams step back to look at the big picture of their results, they can easily identify who requires intensive reteaching, who requires more practice or error analysis, and who requires enrichment or extension. *The Handbook for Collaborative Common Assessments* (Erkens, 2016) contains tools and templates to help teachers strategize next steps once they have identified flexible groupings.

Figure 7.4 serves as an example of data organization with the traditional test. Data can be organized in comparative ways with rubric-based assessments, as well. Figure 7.4 provides an example of common assessment that uses mathematics rubric scores.

In this example, the team assigns each member a label (A–D), and then the individual teacher enters his or her own scores into the spreadsheet under the assigned classroom letter for each of the three learning target areas. Teacher A, for example, knows that student 1 in her classroom is J. Aamon and that learner scored a 3 in Computational Accuracy, a 3 in Communicating Mathematical Thinking, and a 3 in Mathematical Problem Solving.

When teams have a data set such as this one, it is important for them to color-code the numbers to analyze the data. Simple highlighters or autofill colors on a spreadsheet work to layer meaning on top of the numbers (for example, 0s and 1s are red, 2s are yellow, 3s are green, and 4s are left uncolored). When the data are appropriately color-coded, teams can clearly see answers to three important questions.

1. What is the greatest area of growth for the entire team?

2. What is my greatest area of growth as an individual on this team?

3. Which learners need help with which specific learning targets?

Student	Computational Accuracy				Communicating Mathematical Thinking				Mathematical Problem Solving			
	A	B	C	D	A	B	C	D	A	B	C	D
1	3	3	3	4	3	4	2	4	3	4	3	4
2	3	4	3	3	3	3	3	3	3	3	3	3
3	3	3	1	2	3	3	1	3	3	3	1	3
4	3	2	2	3	2	2	2	3	2	2	1	3
5	3	3	3	3	3	2	3	3	3	3	2	2
6	3	2	3	3	3	2	3	3	4	3	2	4
7	2	3	3	3	3	3	2	3	3	2	2	3
8	3	3	2	4	4	3	2	4	4	3	3	3
9	2	3	3	3	3	4	3	3	2	3	3	3
10	3	2	3	1	3	2	3	1	2	1	3	1
11	3	3	3	1	2	2	2	1	3	3	2	1
12	2	2	3	3	3	3	3	2	2	2	3	2
13	3	3	2	3	3	2	3	2	3	2	3	3
14	3	2	2	3	3	2	2	2	3	3	2	2
15	3	3	4	3	3	3	3	3	3	3	3	3
16	3	3	3	2	4	3	3	3	3	3	2	3
17	1	2	2	3	2	3	1	2	1	2	1	2
18	2	3	3	3	2	3	3	3	2	3	2	3
19	2	3	3	3	2	3	3	3	3	3	3	3
20	4	3	2	2	4	3	3	2	3	2	3	3
21	3	3	3	3	3	3	4	3	2	3	4	3
22	2	3	3	3	3	3	3	3	2	3	3	2
23	3	2	3	3	3	3	2	3	3	3	2	3
24	1	2	3	4	1	3	2	4	1	2	3	3
25	2	2	3	3	3	2	2	4	2	1	4	4
Average	2.6	2.7	2.7	2.8	2.8	2.8	2.5	2.8	2.6	2.6	2.5	2.8

Figure 7.4: Common assessment rubric data display by classroom, target, and learner.

Using the system in figure 7.4 will make the patterns emerge for analysis. For example, the most red and yellow will appear in target 3—Mathematical Problem Solving—making that target the greatest area of need for the learners and the greatest area of instructional support for most of the teachers on the team as well.

In this same manner, the team can isolate questions and concerns for individual learners; for example, student 10 in classroom D is scoring a 1 in all three target areas. Now the team can explore the evidence that student 10 has provided to isolate the specific gaps in his or her understanding.

Regardless of the format (percentages, totals, rubric scores, and so on), quantitative data can only signal celebrations and areas of concern. If teams really want to help their learners, they must dig into the evidence to find specifics. They must look at the artifacts or evidence of student learning through both teacher and learner perception. Often, they may have to ask the learner a few questions directly in order to clarify what the learner was thinking as he or she answered—or didn't answer—the questions.

Evidence

Once the data mining reveals the areas that will require deeper exploration, teams use artifacts to find the evidence to prove or disprove the data, as well as to provide deeper insight into the current reality behind the data. Evidence is composed of information gleaned from any assessment artifacts or examples that reveal the learner's work directly. Evidence can be found in teacher observations, a learner's verbal responses (oral or written), and any other information that will corroborate whether an inference, interpretation, or belief teachers form regarding a student's learning can be proven true or valid. Evidence can and should include the learner's own understanding of the types of misconceptions, reasoning errors, or reading errors he or she encountered when engaged in the assessment. Evidence is required to provide confirmation or proof before instructional decisions are made.

Three protocols found in this book's companion, *The Handbook for Collaborative Common Assessments* (Erkens, 2016), support the practice of looking at student work in the context of collaborative common assessments. Each protocol serves a different purpose, and each purpose is very important.

- Calibrate scoring
- Analyze errors
- Refine assessments and measuring tools

A significant reason to analyze student work involves calibrating scoring so that there is consistency and educational equity from classroom to classroom. Teams must engage in the practice of examining student artifacts together on a relatively consistent basis.

Getting Common Data

It is possible for a team to employ a common assessment, but not generate common data. In fact, until teams consistently calibrate their scoring practices, generating *uncommon* data in common situations will be the norm. It is even important to engage in this work with the typical pencil-and-paper test, which is often falsely assumed to be completely objective because there are right and wrong answers. Inconsistent scoring can occur since various scales can be used to score short constructed-response items (for example, "explain your thinking"), or partial credit is offered for wrong answers that reveal simple mistakes but solid thinking in some classrooms, but not in others (for example, "if the learner had not transposed the numbers here, she would have ended up with the right answer").

Certainly, the use of constructed responses or performance assessments, which require the consistent application of scales or rubrics to score proficiency, must be examined collaboratively to guarantee that common data result. Because each teacher will have many learners in a single classroom and because each team has many teachers with the potential of many sections of the same course, the process can quickly become cumbersome and unwieldy without a consistent process and set of tools to review artifacts in a timely manner. Several sampling options are available for teams to use to make the process manageable. The team members must agree in advance which of the following options or combination of options they will use to identify their target subsets.

- **Draw a sample of the students:** Each teacher brings samples of student work from one or more students in the classroom. There are a few alternatives to this method—

    ○ Each teacher brings a random sample comprising the top three to five artifacts from the overall classroom set. (Note: it is important that teachers not preselect an example of a low, middle, or high proficiency level as they will have already entered bias into the scoring conversation; rather, the sample should literally come from the top of the pile. It is feasible that they could select different learners each time they engage in the process.)

    ○ Each teacher brings the work of the exact same one or two learners who have been randomly selected at the outset to each meeting.

- **Draw a sample from the overall expectations:** The team looks at all the work based on a single feature of the assessment expectations (for example, comprehension or content accuracy) or a single criterion (such as organization or sentence fluency).

- **Draw a sample from parts of the products:** The team examines one small section from the entirety of each product (the data charts, the concluding paragraph, number 21 from the test, and so on).

Once the learners have completed the assessment work and the teachers have gathered their agreed-upon samples for scoring, they employ the protocol for calibrating their scoring to be consistent (see this book's companion, *The Handbook for Collaborative Common Assessments* [Erkens, 2016], for a scoring protocol), and within short order the task is completed.

Mining the Artifacts

Teams can do several things to minimize bias and speed the process during their collaborative scoring meeting. First and foremost, it is imperative that teams not bring to the meeting selected artifacts that have been prescored. When the work is prescored, there are three potential negative outcomes: (1) predetermined notions block objectivity; (2) team learning is limited to the initial evaluation of the scorer, so learning conversations are brief and surface level; and (3) safety is compromised as individuals maneuver to protect their personal judgments. Second, individual teachers must cover or remove the names of the learners from their artifacts before the scoring begins. And, finally, teams must engage in blind scoring (for example, each teacher scores each artifact, and each assigned score is hidden until all scoring is completed). Yet another way to increase objectivity involves having individual teachers begin by scoring the work that did not come from their own classrooms. Bias is part of the human condition, and teachers and teams must do all that they can to minimize bias when working with learners.

Once teams have their agreements, their artifacts, and their scoring protocol on the table, they begin scoring the work at the same time, in the same room, with the same tools. It helps if teachers refrain from talking while scoring. Each teacher begins with a sampling that did not come from his or her classroom, a clear set of scoring criteria and guidelines, and small single-colored sticky notes (for example, everyone uses yellow, no one gets a different color) or some other tool on which to record his or her responses. The teacher picks up the student artifact, writes the preferred score on a small note, sticks the score behind the artifact or folds it in a manner so the score cannot be seen by others, and passes it to the next teacher, who also scores it using the same process. Each artifact moves all around the table until all artifacts have been scored.

Once the artifacts have been evaluated by all of the teachers, the team turns them over to reveal the various scores and stacks the artifacts accordingly (for example, all papers scored a 2 go in the two pile, all papers scored a 3 go in the three pile), putting any artifact with different scores on it in the mixed pile. When teams begin this process, the mixed pile is sure to be the tallest pile. Fortunately, the more teams engage in this work, the faster it goes and the more consistent their scoring becomes until there are very few artifacts, if any, in the mixed pile. Once the sorting is done and the piles have been created, the entire team discusses one artifact at a time until the team members come to consensus—not an average—on what the final score will be.

Teams benefit and increase their learning most from the conversation that follows the assigning of scores. The conversation cannot be skipped or abbreviated; it is the conversation that will calibrate everyone's individual scoring to be more consistent. Teachers must hear from each other to clarify terms and expectations, as well as align practices. It would be a mistake, for example, to assume that a paper that generated eight scores of 2 and a single score of 1 during the blind scoring would ultimately be deemed a 2 for the final score. However, as teams deeply explore the criteria and press each other for clarifications, the entire team can shift to agree that the individual who scored the only 1 on that artifact may have scored the most accurately.

After the scores are calibrated for consistency, teachers return to their individual classrooms and score their remaining student work on their own. At this point, they enter their individual data in the agreed-upon format and prepare for the data meeting. Sometimes teachers bring one or two samples of student work unscored to the data meeting to solicit feedback from their colleagues before affixing the final score, but a few papers to score at that point are far more manageable than an entire classroom set.

When teachers thoughtfully and carefully engage in the process of collaborative scoring, they generate consistency in their markings; refine their ability to diagnose misconceptions and errors; enhance their ability to provide focused, target-specific feedback; and improve their own knowledge or skills in a manner that often directly impacts the accuracy, sensitivity, and thoroughness of their instructional responses.

The Missing Link

Teachers require better information to make informed instructional decisions or guide their learning into making their own informed instructional corrections. Typically, traditional undergraduate programs do not prepare teachers to be diagnostic in their evaluations of assessment data, so teachers can struggle with where to turn and how to get better instructional information. Evaluative information alone (such as marks, scores, or grades) does not support quality corrective instruction, so teachers will want to be savvy about diagnosing errors. According to Schneider, Egan, and Julian (2013), "Teachers *rarely* provided thought-provoking feedback that moved students forward in their learning" (pp. 57–58). In the absence of a clear, agreed-upon understanding of types of errors, teachers and learners will likely struggle as they strive to identify and construct instructionally sound responses.

Analyzing Types of Errors

There is a big difference between mistakes and misconceptions or reasoning errors. When learners make mistakes, it usually involves one of three common oversights.

1. Misunderstanding the phrasing of the question

2. Misinterpreting the directions

3. Skipping key words like *not, always,* or *most*

While mistakes show up as *wrong* on the actual assessment, they should not generate considerable attention, feedback, or intervention time (Fisher & Frey, 2012). A teacher can know that the learner is making a mistake when there is alternative, clear evidence that the learner understands the key concepts, terms, or processes.

When a learner makes an error, however, he or she is wrong because of a discernible misunderstanding, a flawed application of a concept or skill, faulty reasoning, or any combination therein. All available evidence demonstrates a visible disconnect between what was taught and what was understood.

Sometimes learners make concept errors. Those errors highlight a misunderstanding of the big idea or specific identifying factors and involve the following.

- Vocabulary concerns or lack of background knowledge

- Preconceived notions

- Gaps in understanding of concepts, skills, or relationships and interactions between and among concepts or skills—

  - Knowledge errors (unclear about definitions)

  - Unable to identify individual parts

  - Unable to explain key processes

  - Unable to link together the interworking relationships

Leading educational experts and authors Douglas Fisher and Nancy Frey (2007) write, "Misconceptions include preconceived notions, nonscientific beliefs, naïve theories, mixed conceptions, or conceptual misunderstandings" (p. 32). So, while concept errors require intervention, the intervention may be as brief and straightforward as providing feedback, engaging learners in self-reflection, or coaching the learner through error analysis. When significant gaps are apparent, reteaching is required, but reassessment may also be needed to further clarify the misconceptions involved.

Sometimes the learners make reasoning errors. A reasoning error involves a faulty or incomplete application of a thinking skill applied to concepts. Some reasoning errors include:

- Misunderstanding the reasoning process
- Employing the reasoning process inaccurately or insufficiently as in the following examples.
  - Unsupported claims
  - Insufficient evidence or sampling errors
  - Overgeneralizations or oversimplifications
  - Inconsistency (in evidence or application)
  - Omissions
  - Contradictions
  - Illogical thinking or non sequitur errors

Like concept errors, reasoning errors almost require interventions. Fisher and Frey (2012) observe:

> Errors occur because of a lack of knowledge. Even when alerted, the learner isn't quite sure what to do to fix the problem. He or she lacks the skills or conceptual understanding to do anything differently when given another opportunity to try. (p. 44)

Learning resides in the gap between confusion and understanding. Errors provide opportunity for deep learning, and those opportunities cannot and should not be missed.

It is easiest to identify the types of errors involved and thus the immediate interventions needed if the learning target is explicitly stated, the team has clear and consistent criteria for quality, the team has samples of student work for reviewing and analyzing, and the team members have the dedicated time, protocols, and templates to support their discussion. *The Handbook for Collaborative Common Assessments* (Erkens, 2016) outlines a protocol for identifying, labeling, and addressing errors. The protocol can be used for straightforward problems with right or wrong answers as well as performance-oriented tasks that require rubrics or scoring guides.

Imagine that a team is working on the skill of drawing conclusions. The teachers begin by clarifying the skill in student-friendly terms: *When reading fiction or nonfiction materials, I draw conclusions. This means I use both implied and stated evidence in and around the text and then form a reasonable judgment or decision about the meaning of the text.* The clarification of terms supports learners in grasping concepts earlier, but it also gives teams clarity around the key details they are seeking in student work.

The team provides a short task for learners to demonstrate their ability to draw conclusions, and the learners provide answers on index cards at the end of the period. The team then gets together and sorts the cards into piles of quality and low-quality conclusions. The teachers then subdivide the group of low-quality conclusions into smaller piles based on specific types of errors that emerge in the student work. They discover that the following errors are at play.

- Conclusion is simply a restatement of an explicit piece of text evidence.

- Conclusion is based on faulty or inappropriate evidence.

- Conclusion is based on singular or insufficient evidence and misses the complete picture.

- There is sufficient or accurate evidence, but the conclusion is based on weak reasoning or faulty logic.

The team members seek to identify the common patterns or anomalies in the evidence so that they themselves can draw conclusions regarding the most prevalent mistakes and errors.

Collaborative Common Assessments in Action: Analyzing Errors

During a unit on balancing chemical reactions, a high school science department put the following bell-ringer activity on the board:

Balance the equation $H_2O_2 \rightarrow H_2O + O_2$

The teachers gave their students an index card as they entered the room and asked the students to take their seats and individually begin solving the problem posted on the board. After five minutes, each teacher gathered the notecards and quickly sorted the cards into "right" and "wrong" piles, making sure no student's name or work was revealed as he or she did so. Each teacher then selected a card that did something right but made a common error. Teachers rewrote the card they had selected in their own handwriting so no student would be identified and then used the projector to show the work and engaged the classroom in addressing the following questions:

- What are all of the things that were done properly or well in this example?
- What error was made? What evidence indicates that error was made?
- How do we fix that type of error?

In one of the classrooms, Teacher A selected a card that did a few things correct, but had a common error on it. She selected her favorite example from the wrong pile and rewrote it so that it was in her own handwriting, and titled it her "favorite no":

$$H_22O_2 \rightarrow H_22O + O_2$$

After identifying all that was right about the work, the students moved into analyzing what was wrong with the current answer.

- Error: The learner put the coefficients in the wrong place.
- Correct answer was $2H_2O_2 \rightarrow 2H_2O + O_2$

The team met at the end of the day to compare *all* of their error cards (even the ones they did not use during the lesson) so they could isolate trends and anomalies and also problem solve the instructional next steps to address the types of errors students made.

The team agreed the quick formative assessment was powerful and supported the learning for both teachers and students alike. The team members noted that all of their students seemed willing and able to join in with addressing errors quickly. They also observed over time that the practice of examining errors as a whole class led students to grasp concepts more quickly and autocorrect more independently and more consistently. As a collaborative formative assessment, the process was easy, manageable, and rewarding.

Errors are not always easily identified. Teams must work together to analyze and appropriately diagnose errors.

Error Analysis to Target Learning Needs

When collaborative common assessments are formative in nature and error analysis is involved, teams can make robust instructional decisions to close learning gaps prior to the summative assessment. Teams use quick data to make agile decisions about the appropriate instructional fixes for each of the existing types of errors. In the previous example regarding common errors with drawing conclusions, it is clear that reteaching the definition of drawing conclusions will not help the learners who are not identifying sufficient or accurate evidence. The strategies a team selects to address specific types of errors will have to be different to address the specific needs of that group of learners. It is a waste of precious resources to engage learners in interventions that they do not require. If they enter the conversation already understanding the concepts or skills being retaught, the intervention is disrespectful and ineffective. Those learners require coaching and the opportunity to conduct their own error analysis so they can focus on precision and revision strategies.

Figure 7.5 offers an example of the powerful and instructionally sensitive data that teams can generate when they use collaborative formative assessments to analyze errors.

Results of drawing conclusions exit slip:
- Four participating classrooms with one hundred completed exit cards
- Seventy-four accurate cards
- Five mistakes
- Twenty-one errors

Number of cards	Mistake or error	Classrooms	Students
5	Skipped key words in passage	A, B, C	JN, BV, RE, HY, WD
5	Restated explicit text	A, C, D	KL, MN, SA, FR, CV
7	Faulty or inappropriate evidence	A, B, C, D	KJ, OP, BR, CD, BG, LO, TG
8	Singular or insufficient evidence	A, C, D	BT, AG, WN, JT, LI, EF, BY, FS
2	Weak reasoning or faulty logic	B, D	KL, TR

Figure 7.5: Identifying errors in common formative assessments.

Once the evidence is gathered and the errors are identified, the team can begin designing instructional interventions to align with each type of error. One powerful intervention option is to have teachers select strong examples of errors that did not come from their individual classrooms and (after blocking all student names so no learner is revealed in the process) then ask learners to engage in the very same sorting and piling process to see if they can isolate errors, name them, and identify possible strategies to address such types of errors.

In a robust, balanced assessment system, learners take an active role in monitoring their results and making instructional decisions. To participate in that manner, they must self-regulate. According to professor and researcher Heidi Andrade (2013), "in general, the regulation of learning involves four main processes: (1) goal-setting, (2) the monitoring of progress toward the goal, (3) interpretation of feedback derived from monitoring, and (4) adjustment of goal-directed action including, perhaps, redefining the goal itself" (p. 21). To do so, learners require better data, and collaborative common assessments can easily provide learners with the opportunity to engage in that manner.

When teams design their assessment, they start with designing the architectural blueprint behind the assessment. Once the assessment is actually designed, teams convert the architectural blueprint into a ready-to-use student reflection form. The form is withheld until after the learners have taken the assessment. If the reflection form is set up the right way, teachers can save time in their marketing efforts and simultaneously gather significant evidence regarding the students' perspectives on their individual performances. In this situation, less is more. Less feedback can actually generate additional quality evidence that informs next steps.

Imagine that the team members give their assessment at the end of the week. Teachers individually score their classroom set, but the work is far easier and less time-consuming than is normally done. Rather than fixing errors inside the test with notations; counting the number of correct answers; generating percentages, totals, or grades at the top of the test; and then putting those results in the gradebook, the teacher simply places a dot next to the number of any question that is wrong. When the student returns to the classroom, the teacher gives the learner his or her test with dots on it and the accommodating reflection form. The student will use the reflection form to conduct his or her own analysis of the results. The student fills in the reflection form, computes the number correct for each target area, and then makes instructional decisions about what must come next in the learning. Figure 7.6 (pages 124–125) shows the reflection form for student O in classroom E that would have accommodated the earlier assessment results from the common assessment on information literacy.

If learners are the instructional decision makers, then they must be actively engaged in monitoring their own progress and setting goals for themselves. In every assessment they take, learners should be able to identify as many strengths (if not more) as opportunities to grow and improve. In healthy assessment systems and practices, "a key feature . . . is that students occupy a central and active role in all feedback processes, including and especially monitoring

Goal Setting

Student O, Classroom E

Item	Target	Mark Wrong (X)	Simple Mistake or Still Learning	Results and Resources
1	Locate Information			I have __5__ out of 6 correct.
2	Locate Information	X	Reading error	What will you do?
3	Locate Information			____ Keep working
4	Locate Information			_X_ Done
5	Locate Information			
6	Locate Information			

Possible Resources: LA text pages 212–215; A 2 and A 3 folder handouts on 5 Ws and How

Item	Target	Mark Wrong (X)	Simple Mistake or Still Learning	Results and Resources
7	Explain Purpose			I have __6__ out of 6 correct.
8	Explain Purpose			What will you do?
9	Explain Purpose			____ Keep working
10	Explain Purpose			_X_ Done
11	Explain Purpose			
12	Explain Purpose			

Possible Resources: LA text pages 219–221 and any variety of texts for reading

Item	Target	Mark Wrong (X)	Simple Mistake or Still Learning	Results and Resources
13	Analyze Differences			I have __6__ out of 6 correct.
14	Analyze Differences			What will you do?
15	Analyze Differences			____ Keep working
16	Analyze Differences			_X_ Done
17	Analyze Differences			
18	Analyze Differences			

Possible Resources: LA text pages 222–227 and source reliability lab and tools (all C folders)

Item	Target	Mark Wrong (X)	Simple Mistake or Still Learning	Results and Resources
19	Assess Evidence			I have __2__ out of 7 correct.
20	Assess Evidence	X	Reading error	What will you do?
21	Assess Evidence			_X_ Keep working
22	Assess Evidence	X	Concept error	____ Done
23	Assess Evidence	X	Reading error	
24	Assess Evidence	X	Concept error	
25	Assess Evidence	X	Reasoning	

Possible Resources: LA text pages 228–230 and Crime Lab for Linguistic Evidence

Item	Target	Mark Wrong (X)	Simple Mistake or Still Learning	Results and Resources
26–30	Organize and Communicate Rubric item: Organize—5-point scale: 2 points	X	Concept and reasoning errors	I have __2__ out of 10 correct. What will you do? _X_ Keep working ____ Done
31–35	Organize and Communicate Rubric item: Communicate—5-point scale: 0 points	X	Concept and reasoning errors	
Possible Resources: LA text pages 232–237 and writing rubrics				

Goal Setting

Reference your data to answer these questions.

My strengths (the targets I learned):

My areas for growth (the targets I am still learning):

My learning goal:

Evidence I will generate to indicate I have met my learning goal:

Sources: Chappuis, 2014; Chappuis et al., 2012; Vagle, 2015.

Figure 7.6: Student reflection form.

and regulating their progress toward desired goals and evaluating the efficacy of the strategies used to reach those goals" (Andrade, 2013, p. 21).

The reflection forms that learners use provide the invaluable information that learners require to remain motivated and become successful, as well as additional information for teachers who must now intervene regarding the results. Often, when teachers understand what the learners were thinking and feeling during the experience of the assessment, they themselves can make better choices regarding best next steps.

Data meetings benefit teachers and their learners. No matter who examines the data, the experience should be synergistic and enlightening. Data mining and the resulting insights should invite, if not compel, individuals to want to improve their practice.

The work of collaborative common assessments helps teachers and their learners self-regulate to improve. Each and every data encounter should invite learning and provide opportunities for those engaged to experience flow in their daily work. Data conversations at every level must provide insights and information that ultimately generate commitment and the motivation to carry on.

8

Responding With Instructional Agility

Power has to be insecure to be responsive.

—Ralph Nader

If collaborative common assessments are not improving the core of instruction, then they are not working. Teachers cannot remain steadfast in their instructional practices while making the learners adapt. Assessment must be a diagnostic process that provides teacher and learner alike with plausible next steps. Sometimes it feels as if organizations collect and display data for the simple reason that it's expected. Collecting data for the sake of data is a waste of everyone's precious time and resources. If learning communities are going to take the time to gather data, it must be for the purposes of answering the difficult questions *What will we do for the students who have not yet learned it?* and *What will we do for the students who already have it?* Teams must use common assessment data to support their individual and collective mastery, to make program improvements, and to respond in instructionally agile ways.

Figure 8.1 (page 128) demonstrates the part of the collaborative common assessment process in which teams must make decisions that are responsive to the data and the resulting conclusions regarding their findings.

Program improvement intersects with both the original instructional cycle and the intervention instructional cycle. Program improvements are tied to the process of each cycle, and the insights learned from each cycle can inform the work of the other cycle. Intervention planning starts the pathway to a new cycle of instruction. If teams commit to the belief that learning is required, then instructionally agile intervention systems are required at the individual classroom level, the team level, and the entire school level.

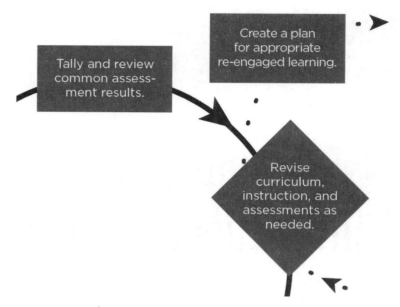

Figure 8.1: Program improvement and intervention planning.

Making Program Improvements

In the absence of comparative data, teachers struggle to make program improvements. Without data, decisions are based on personal and professional opinion, and individuals within the department or grade level often disagree. Whether a program improves is left to the discretion of the individual until the district steps in and insists on new curricular resources, purchases new assessments, or requires the application of specific instructional strategies. Figure 8.2 outlines the work that teams must do as they mine data so they can respond appropriately with instruction.

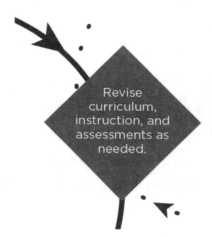

Figure 8.2: Program improvement decision making.

When teams have collaborative data, they can make program improvements at the classroom level. And when teams don't have accessible data, they can commit to using the collaborative common assessment process to gather the data before making decisions. Of course, they may not have the budget at the team level for purchasing choices, but they have the option to make different or improved decisions within their locus of control.

Curriculum

A curriculum is defined as the materials and means educators use to bring the standards to life in their classrooms. Curriculum includes all of the various resources (textbooks, videos, supplemental articles, interviews, and so on) that teachers use with learners to help them understand the standards. While teams might not have the money or power to purchase major curriculum resources, like updated textbooks, they certainly have the option—and most likely the need—to remove, supplement, or modify those things found within their printed textbook materials, especially if their data suggest that learners need something more, or different, to achieve the standards successfully. Today, it is already clear that teachers are going to need to do more things with primary sources, digital sources, and technical reading materials with higher Lexile levels if they are to hit the demands of 21st century skills and next-generation standards. In a global society and the information era, curricula must be so much broader than a single textbook.

When teams review common assessment data, they must isolate the variables that may have led to or distracted from their overall success. Curriculum is an input measure that becomes one variable teams must explore. For example, on a third-grade language arts test about classification, the team members explored the data and quickly realized the curriculum could be linked to two of their assessment findings: (1) the language provided in the unit used basic words like *snakes*, but the language provided on the unit test used more complex words like *reptiles*, and many of their learners failed questions when they came upon words that had not been part of the curriculum preparatory materials; and (2) the assessment for the unit required learners to create their own classification based on something they had read, yet nowhere in the previous curricular resources were learners asked to create their own classification. The gaps in the curricular resources created bias in the assessment.

When large-scale assessment took shape in the 1980s, it became clear that when teachers moved at what they believed was the pace of learning, they weren't making it through the necessary curriculum. In direct response, education began requiring teachers to use textbooks and follow pacing guides with fidelity. The practice of turning pacing guides into rules rather than tools once served a purpose: making sure learners were exposed to the entire curriculum so they would be ready for the following year. Too often, that practice has actually prohibited learning. Oliver Wendell Holmes once said, "I would not give a fig for the simplicity this side of complexity, but I would give my life for the simplicity on the other side of complexity ("Oliver Wendell Holmes Sr.," 2015). Navigating curriculum is a complex process, and removing decision making from teachers oversimplifies the work and under-empowers the key decision makers who are closest to the front lines. It's true that individual teachers should not be able to unilaterally decide what they will and will not teach, and the standards are nonnegotiable. So, teams of teachers must work together to tackle the complex problem of helping their learners attain mastery on all of the standards while strategically moving at the true pace of learning.

Collaborative Common Assessments in Action: Using Data to Shape Curriculum

Nai-ma asked her eighth-grade team of teachers to consider teaching social studies by process rather than by era as they had been doing. Her colleagues were not receptive to the idea. They felt what they had always done was working. They neither wanted to spend the energy to make the shift nor wanted to run the risk that they would be less successful if they made the change. But Nai-ma, who had experienced teaching social studies by process in another country, knew of a better way, and she would not be satiated by complacency born out of comfort.

She persisted: "I don't want to teach by opinion. Let's go get the data! How about if we continue as we have been for the rest of this semester—teaching social studies by era—and we use this time to gather evidence from our common assessments regarding the students' depth of knowledge. I commit to lead the curriculum design work for next semester. Let's continue our work with common assessments next semester using the new curriculum, and then we can compare results regarding which way works best." The team agreed to her terms.

The team noted positive changes early in the process of switching to the new curriculum. Even without a full semester's worth of data, the team quickly observed learners were better able to retain information and contextualize content. Nai-ma knew the only way to win that argument was from the point of data and not from the place of personal opinion or experience.

Instruction

The work of collaborative common assessments is rooted in *understanding* instruction. A team is strong when it is inquiry based and instructionally diverse and agile. One person cannot do it all, and student success should not be limited to the luck of the draw regarding teacher prowess.

Master teachers can accomplish *learning* through instruction in less time than average teachers, yet they often cannot describe their craft knowledge. Mastery always involves depth of knowledge and fluidity of skill. For master teachers, their understanding of instruction is often based in tacit knowledge. University professors and authors Han Sik Shim and Gene Roth (2008) note:

> A key difference between expert teachers and novice teachers resides not in "what they do" (their content knowledge), but with the "how they do" (their procedural knowledge). Expert teaching professors possess tacit knowledge of how they do their job, but if they are like other types of expert workers, they may struggle in their attempts to surface this knowledge and explain it to others. (p. 5)

The collaborative common assessment process requires teams to explore their past instructional findings and future instructional implications. Teams need to be able to look backward as well as forward regarding what instruction or instructional strategies to keep, modify, or drop. Collaborative common assessments help teams unpack the art and science of teaching, creating a local research base of what works.

Collaborative Common Assessments in Action: Tracking Data to Empower Teams

As an elementary school intervention specialist, Cal wanted to make sure that he was not managing all of the intervention work, thereby overhelping and under-empowering the teams. He wanted to make sure that as an intervention specialist, he was strengthening the core of intervention at the classroom level, too. He decided that he would participate in all of the grade-level data team meetings, but his role would need to be different than it had been in the past. Moving forward, he would share intervention strategies, participate in problem solving, engage in gathering data, and most importantly, act as the on-site researcher regarding what instructional strategies worked and which ones didn't. In each of the major literacies— reading, writing, and mathematics—he created an open, digital database that everyone could see and anyone could contribute to. He set the database up to track the following.

- Grade level

- Content and learning targets

- Common errors for each target area

- The list or types of available assessments at their disposal to monitor the desired content or process (comprehension, fluency, and so on)

- The measuring tools, quality indicators, and proficiency levels that best served as the appropriate performance indicators

- The specific intervention tools or resources the team committed to try

- The resulting data (effectiveness) of that intervention tool or resource

Cal then tracked the number and sequence of the interventions (what happened first, second, third, and so on, and what impact on student success each impact seemed to have).

Each database began to look somewhat like a sports-related tournament bracket, filled with if-then criteria wherein some instructional strategies advanced as winners, but others did not. Cal wanted to make sure the teams were the ones who made the decisions and did the work. He would record their work and maintain a clear and present support role, but he knew it was imperative that he empower the team and ultimately strengthen core instruction. Prevention, he believed, was so much better than intervention.

Assessment

There is no such thing as a perfect or bias-free assessment. Many times, flaws in student achievement are a result of the assessment itself and not the curriculum, the instruction, or the learner. Given the disconnect between curriculum-based assessments and standards, or the lack of assessment literacy in quality design, errors in assessment design could likely be the most common program error in regard to student achievement. Still, the issue of assessment design must be reserved for last in the list of program-based discussions for improvement. When assessment issues lead the conversation, teachers accidently end up watering down the rigor of the assessment design so that future learners might be successful when, in truth, the failure in student achievement may have been a curriculum- or instruction-based error. Only after teams have discussed curriculum- or instruction-based errors should they turn their attention to the assessment design—unless, of course, the design flaw is blatantly obvious early on.

If the assessment results can be tied to assessment design flaws, then learners should not be held accountable for the flaws. Teaching teams would have to agree to ignore the data regarding the outcome of their flawed question, task, prompt, or attendant measuring tool. When errors are assessment design–based, the incredible conversations that support teacher learning with accurate assessment design and effective use can happen.

Collaborative Common Assessments in Action: Learning From Assessment Errors

The teachers on a mathematics team noticed that the majority of their learners missed question 19 on the test. After exploring the curricular instructional implications in their data, the team members turned their attention to question 19 to see if they could analyze what went wrong. They discovered confusion in their own directions. The test item was set up so that a series of eight shapes, each with an assigned letter, ran across the page. The item required learners to identify which of the shapes matched the criteria provided on each of four lines. The directions failed to mention that a shape could be used on more than one line and that each shape could be referenced more than once. Following that discovery, the team engaged in a rigorous debate regarding whether or not it was fair to withhold information from test-takers, and whether or not it was an accurate assessment of brilliance to wait and see which learners figured it out on their own. In the end, the team decided that an assessment should not be filled with secrets or surprises; rather, learners always needed a clear indication of what was expected of them. The conversation was rigorous, and it helped shape the team's approach to future assessment design.

Better Assessment Designs

If the results are tied to the types of common errors that learners make, then the team can create strong assessment designs for next steps. Future assessments regarding the content area can become more diagnostic in nature. Andrade (2013) states that "diagnostic questions can also be implemented in the form of multiple-choice items. . . . Multiple-choice items . . . can provide diagnostic information to teachers about student understanding [when the items are based on construct maps]" (p. 18). Imagine, for example, that a team had the following learning target: *When reading, I use both implied and stated evidence in and around the text and then form a reasonable judgment or decision about the meaning of the text.* Then, following the use of a common formative assessment, the team members discovered the following common errors in the practice of drawing conclusions.

- A simple restatement
- Faulty or inappropriate evidence
- Singular or insufficient evidence
- Weak reasoning or faulty logic

So, they designed assessment items that included the types of errors as plausible distractors. That way, when the learner selected the error, the teachers were able to identify the type of mistake being made. Figure 8.3 outlines an example of a test item that includes errors as plausible distractors.

Read the quotation below. Select the answer that draws an accurate conclusion.
"The teacher, pinching her brow into dark lines of disgust, told them to show respect."

    a. The kids are annoying the instructor because of their behavior (correct answer).

    b. The teacher is trying to remove extra eyebrow hair (incorrect: misinterpreted evidence: pinching brow).

    c. The teacher is pinching her brow (incorrect: restate explicit evidence).

    d. Teachers get mad when kids laugh too much (incorrect: overgeneralized, not tied to specific evidence).

For even more clarity regarding student errors, the team added the following questions.

1. Which answer is the right answer _____, and what clues do you have that suggest it is the right answer?	Clues:
2. Which answer uses an explicit statement _____, and what would be wrong with that answer?	Explain:
3. Which answer is overgeneralized _____, and what would be wrong with that answer?	Word(s):

Figure 8.3: Sample test item with plausible distractors with drawing conclusions.

Developing better test questions using errors can be accomplished in every discipline. Figure 8.4 provides an example of using errors to create plausible distractors in mathematics.

Program improvements are critical to any organization's success. Schools must constantly monitor what works and what needs improvement. When collaborative common assessments are used, teams must examine their curriculum, instruction, and assessments to make data-based, program-improvement decisions.

Target: I can round when making decisions that involve numbers. This means I increase or decrease a number to get to the next shortened number that will help me make the best decision.

Common errors:

- Not rounding at all
- Increasing or decreasing without creating a shortened number
- Rounding only by rule
- Rounding the wrong direction

Sample Question With Plausible Distractors:

1. For our spring trip to Wolf Ridge, we will need school buses to transport the students. A school bus holds 36 students. If we have 269 students to be transported, how many buses will we need? _____ (C)

   A. 7 (incorrect: rounding by rule)

   B. 7.47 (incorrect: exact mathematics, no rounding)

   C. 8 (correct: rounding with reasoning)

   D. 8.47 (incorrect: exact mathematics with reasoning to increase number but missing the concept of rounding all together; note: another response with ".47" is required to create a balance to the homogeneous look of the overall responses)

Engaging learners in error analysis:

- What's the right answer?
- Explain what makes the answer you selected the best answer.
- Pick an answer you didn't select and explain the type of error it's making.
    - Letter: _____   Error Made: _____

Figure 8.4: Sample test item with plausible distractors with rounding.

Planning Instructional Responses

Learning does not happen at the same pace and in the same way for all learners. For that reason, it is imperative that teachers support—without judgment or frustration—learners who did not succeed the first time.

Sharon Kramer (2015) notes that learners require the utmost respect when engaged in the learning process:

> When students struggle, it is not respectful to ask them to do the same activity over while the teacher says it louder and slower. Re-engagement rather than mere reteaching is what students need. While reteaching involves teaching the unit lessons over again, re-engaging analyzes student errors and missteps and asks students to revisit their thinking. It is also not respectful to ask students who have demonstrated proficiency to do even more of the same work. Therefore, respectful re-engaging is high-interest, engaging, and appropriately challenging for all students. (p. 22)

In the United States, response to intervention (RTI) legislation demands schools engage in processes that monitor how well students respond to changes in instruction or interventions. The three-tiered pyramid model requires educators to develop and use an evidence-based assessment system for monitoring student learning integrated with a multitiered, research-based instructional response system to ensure all learners achieve at high levels. The goal is to engage staff in the collaborative monitoring of *all* learners and to increase academic success by intervening with instructional agility.

In essence, the work of collaborative common assessment forms the base, otherwise known as Tier 1 of the RTI model. Tier 1 involves universal instruction, which according to legislation, should address 80 percent of the identified learning needs during or in response to instruction. The interventions at Tier 1 should be addressed through core instruction directly within the classroom, catching learners before the discrepancy becomes so great as to be insurmountable. It is only when Tier 1 re-engagement with universal instructional strategies does not work that learners progress to Tier 2 for targeted instruction with additional resources, scientifically based interventions, and frequent progress monitoring. Very few—approximately 5 percent—of the learners should ever advance to Tier 3 for intensive instruction, with the support of multiple experts to intervene and monitor progress weekly. Figure 8.5 illustrates how the common assessment process engages teams in using their common assessment results to diagnose specific learning needs and then respond accordingly at the classroom level.

Unfortunately, many schools create Tier 1 options that are actually more aligned to Tier 2 targeted interventions, and as a result, learners are immediately moved to the care of intervention specialists hired to assume responsibility for struggling learners, having little impact on core instruction and the general education classroom. Likewise, the planned responses are typically more like interventions than re-engagement strategies, and they do not always provide the appropriate corrective instruction. As it has been implemented in most educational settings, the RTI system often falls short of accomplishing either of its primary goals of responding with *targeted* interventions and improving the core of instruction. Dylan Wiliam (2013) notes:

> RTI seems to be based on a very limited view of feedback. In the RTI model, the elicitation of evidence is generally just a form of monitoring whether students are making the progress expected. While monitoring of student progress can identify which students are not making the expected progress, there is a disconnect between the evidence elicitation and the consequent action. All the monitoring assessment does is to identify that the original instruction was not effective and something else needs to be tried, but the evidence listed does not indicate what kinds of alternative intervention should be tried. (p. 211)

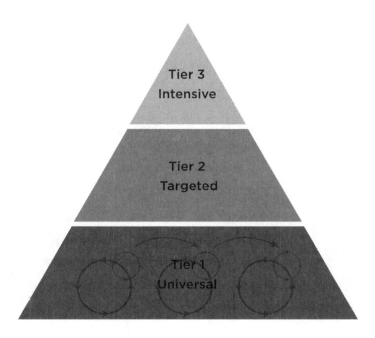

Figure 8.5: Collaborative common assessments in the RTI model.

Learning communities must examine their assessment results deeply to better diagnose the learners' needs and then create specific, targeted re-engagement opportunities. They must monitor the effectiveness of their instructional responses in a manner that not only guarantees all learners are successful, but also that the core of their instruction improves almost daily. In other words, educators must think and act like scientists as they solve the complex problem of ensuring mastery for all.

Differentiated Responses

It stands to reason that the most important role of teams following a data conversation involves planning the instructional responses for *all* of the learners. Each process that is used must be delivered with the utmost care and respect for the learners, whether they require enrichment or re-engagement. The Professional Learning Community at Work experts, DuFour, DuFour, and Eaker (2008), assert that when working as a PLC, teams must respond to their data findings by answering two questions.

1. What will we do for the students who did not master the expectations?

2. What will we do for the students who have mastered the expectations?

In the collaborative common assessment process, those questions are addressed in the smaller circle found in figure 8.6 (page 138).

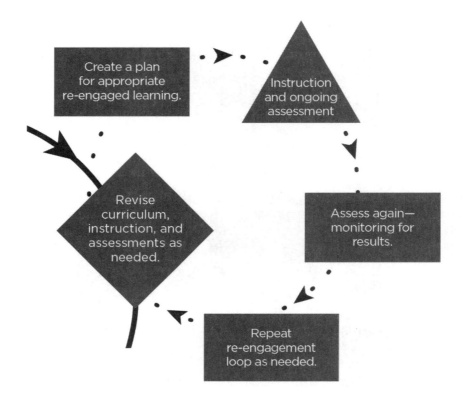

Figure 8.6: Response cycle.

If the school believes that learning is required, and some learners have not yet been successful, then planning for re-engagement in the learning is imperative to a school's and learners' success. Because the final question is about enrichment and extension, it does not feel as critical for teams to address; yet, too many learners do not reach their full potential while they remain in a holding pattern for everyone to get caught up. *Both* questions require instructional agility and responsiveness. Teams must work together to differentiate their instruction (DuFour et al., 2012; DuFour & Mattos, 2013; Hattie, 2009; Kramer, 2015). Figure 8.7 illustrates the tiered instructional responses that happen simultaneously as teams respond to their findings.

The processes are similar, though not exact, for re-engaging learners in the core concepts and conducting error analysis and coaching for those who require minimal adjustments, but the process is different for enrichment, as teachers provide neither direct instruction nor reassess opportunities. Extension opportunities are intended to support learning that is *already mastered* by increasing the challenge opportunity in a rewarding and exciting way, so the resulting enrichment project (product or performance) provides the indication of learning.

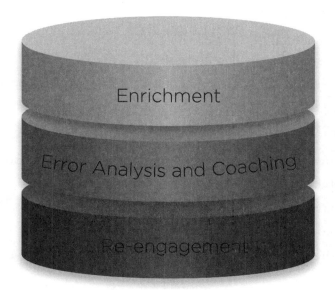

Figure 8.7: Tiered instructional responses to collaborative common assessment results.

Differentiating instruction is challenging work. It works best when a team of teachers creates multiple engaging instructional pathways that will captivate learners' interests; leverages the learners' knowledge, skills, abilities, and talents; maximizes individual potential; and then shares the responsibility of ensuring mastery for all. The tiered response process should not be considered a laborious add-on to direct instruction:

> Differentiation is not a set of strategies but is instead a way of thinking about the teaching and learning process. Differentiation is not about who will learn what but rather how will you teach so that all students have access to, and support and guidance in, mastering the district and state curriculum. (Kramer, 2015, p. 17)

Differentiation works best when navigated from a proactive stance—from beginning to ending—as a way of conducting instruction.

When teams differentiate by learner, by target, and by instructional strategy, they find themselves truly engaged in flexible grouping rather than ability grouping. From unit to unit, different learners will be engaged in different instructional response processes. No matter the process the learner requires, teams must commit to respond with kindness and the utmost respect for the learner (Kramer, 2015). Learning is challenging and risky business. Every learner deserves a teacher's best efforts, no matter the learner's needs. Says Kramer (2015), "The goal is to plan respectful tasks—which include high expectations for all students with activities that equally engage each learner" (p. 22). It is always important to remember that when educational labels are attached to learners, it is solely for the purposes of helping educators make better and more informed decisions to support those learners; it is *never* for the purposes of labeling and then boxing learners into prescribed categories. Differentiation is about creating equity, not equality, in the classroom. There is nothing more inequitable than treating everyone as equal.

Problem Solving When Learning Doesn't Happen

Sometimes, a learner may not have completed the learning expectations in the allotted time frame. When that happens, teams must respond in a manner that supports continued learning, especially in a school system that asserts learning is required. All learners will fall into this category at times, and educators must treat struggling learners with respect, compassion, and keen attention to the root cause.

If learners have opted to behave as intentional nonlearners, then the school must provide a pathway (homework lunch, before-school study halls, and so on) that requires learning and that may become more restrictive over time with repeat offenders (such as increasing loss of privileges with intentional nonlearners). Even then, learners deserve respect and patience as they strive to become responsible adults. When things don't work as they should, it often says less about the individual and more about the system involved. When learners opt out of learning, it is a system problem, not a people problem.

Albert Einstein once noted that yesterday's solutions become tomorrow's problems. Second-chance testing—the space in which learners can retake an assessment because learning is required and time is a variable—has become part of a new problem.

Eliminating the Game Playing of Second-Chance Testing

With a focus on learning rather than teaching, many schools have adopted policies that include second-chance testing for their learners. Learners are playing a game regarding second-chance testing: they are not applying themselves the first time because they know they have a second chance (and possibly many more chances). It might seem that this visible and annoying trait would reflect negatively on the learners (*they are just playing games,* or *they don't take their learning seriously,* or *they just don't care anymore*); but in truth, it is more accurately a negative reflection on the assessment system that has been implemented. It is human nature to take the path of least resistance, and even adults take that same path if provided the option.

Teachers and schools can do some specific and strategic things to avoid second-chance testing abuse for learners who prefer to play the new game. For instance, before the first summative assessment, it is essential that teachers create the systems that provide encouragement for students to get things right the first time.

- Begin every unit of instruction by clearly stating the learning expectations up front. Learners cannot hit a target that they cannot see. Showing learners the expectations provides them with a road map of where they are headed and the signposts to monitor along the way.

- Begin every unit of instruction by clearly indicating what the enrichment or extension opportunities will involve.

- Employ high-quality, meaningful formative assessments along the way. In this arena, quality trumps quantity. It is more important that teachers make sure the assessments they design and employ will generate meaningful data to guide instructional decisions than it is to have an excess of data points in the online gradebook. Formative assessments are intended to help learners and teachers decide what comes next in learning. When it comes to making high-quality instructional decisions, focused information found in a manageable number of data points will work best. Teachers must tie their specific learning targets to each and every question or task found in the formative assessments to get such meaningful data.

- Engage learners in tracking progress throughout the unit of instruction learning target by learning target so that they can make careful and strategic instructional decisions about where and how to invest their time to best prepare for the summative assessment. When students can easily see they have mastered learning targets 1–3 and 5, but they are still making some errors with targets 4 and 6, they can do a better job of focusing their attention and even doubling their efforts to guarantee readiness for the summative assessment. Even young students from kindergarten up can keep track of their learning when given the right information and tools with which to track it.

  - Don't ask students to track grades or points on the assessments leading into the summative assessment. Grades and points hide too many realities about what's happening inside the results they demonstrated regarding their learning. For example, a learner can be generating relatively high scores on his or her assignments and still be bombing an entire strand of a specific learning expectation. More importantly, astute learners who can see they are missing the mark can't fix their errors just based on points. Instead, they require information (feedback) about the types of errors they are making and the potential strategies or skills to fix those types of errors. Points and grades dilute the learning issues at hand.

  - Don't ask learners to track their data if they won't be allowed to use their data in meaningful ways. Data for the sake of data are never helpful, so provide learners with the opportunity to use their data to make strategic decisions. If a learner proves competency over a learning target, should he or she have to continue doing all of the practice work with that target? One way to increase motivation to get things right the first time is to have right the first time count toward something meaningful. Getting out of additional work—especially if it is guaranteed to be busy work—is always meaningful to learners and teachers!

After the first chance but before the second, it is essential to require additional support that demands continued learning, *but does not punish the learner for making mistakes the first time.* The trick is to make the additional support between assessments meaty enough to require time and energy but not punitive in a manner that shames the learners who weren't trying to slide by in the first place and who truly need the additional instruction and help. Even adults don't all learn at the same rates. What is important is that in the end, everyone learns all that was expected. If learners are sliding by—awaiting second chances to take assessments—and they learn that there is additional learning required on their part, they are less likely to slide by the first time.

Managing Support Between Assessments

Additional support systems between assessments require, first and foremost, new and different instruction. Re-engagement should be based specifically on the types of errors learners were making during the initial learning and in that first summative assessment. If the error in understanding or reasoning is not addressed directly and corrected instructionally, then more opportunities to fill in packets simply provide learners with more opportunities to practice it incorrectly yet again, and practice makes *permanent,* not perfect.

It's best to create a multitiered support system that employs the genius of *and*: teachers must provide continued coaching, reteaching, or re-engagement activities, *and* learners must set specific goals regarding targeted areas needing improvement and then initiate additional learning strategies and efforts (beyond the teacher's efforts) to address their own learning needs and goals.

When teachers design interventions, the work must be mandatory and not voluntary for *all* learners who did not master the given expectations. Learning is required. The work can—and should—be available to those who passed but still wish to hit mastery in a given target area. Teachers provide coaching, reteaching, or re-engagement activities that:

- Employ a laser-like focus on specific targets and the accompanying errors

- Require additional learning

- Will generate new work on behalf of the involved learners

Let's look at the specific ways coaching, reteaching, and re-engagement can provide support to struggling learners.

Coaching

When learners make simple mistakes on the first summative assessment, their in-between assessment work involves conducting error analysis on their own work. Because these learners have enough substance upon which to build, they need to be isolating patterns in their work, identifying strategies that address errors so they can avoid falling into that pattern again. Sometimes, looking at samples of strong and weak work and practicing scoring that work can be helpful.

Reteaching and Re-engaging Learners to Support Their Self-Investment

When learners make significant errors in concepts or reasoning, re-engagement and error analysis will likely not suffice. Because learners who make concept and reasoning errors do not have enough of a base on which to build, the teacher must conduct the error analysis and then target the intervention to reteach the specific gaps in knowledge and reasoning. When learners are required to engage in the work of interventions (or they choose to improve their levels of proficiency), they must start with their own self-assessment and goal setting.

After the second summative assessment, the data must be mined once more to either verify learning or diagnose patterns and anomalies. It is important to certify mastery against standards, so *when* a student attains mastery is not significant; *that* a student attains mastery is significant. Sometimes, more teaching and assessment will be required. Teams must examine the learning expectations and the learner's needs carefully so as to make thoughtful decisions as to how many times to engage or re-engage in coaching or reteaching before advancing instruction or before making a choice to move the learner further up on the pyramid of response to intervention.

Deciding When to Advance Learning

Making decisions about when to advance learning is never algorithmic. Odd policies are created that indicate a teacher should move forward with the learning expectations when 80 percent or more of the students have mastered the content. In truth, the decision to move forward with instruction is far more complex than a simple algorithm, and it requires critical thinking, focused problem solving, and the collective wisdom of committed experts. Decisions are oversimplified when they are reduced to single factors like *numbers of learners ready to move.* The numbers factor plays a role in decision making, but it cannot be the defining factor when there are still struggling learners in the classroom. If a learner is still struggling, there are a host of criteria to consider.

- Is the issue at hand one of skill or one of will? (Educators must be careful not to default to the natural inclination that the issue is one of will, or resistance on behalf of the learner to succeed.)

- Is learning imperative for success at the next level?

- Are there multiple points of evidence to verify readiness for the learners who are perceived to be ready to move forward? Are the data accurate? Thorough?

- Is it important that everyone has *mastery*, or can *informed* be sufficient to move forward?

- Can the learning expectations still missing for some learners be successfully scaffolded into future opportunities?

- Can a team of teachers or intervention specialists intervene with a small group and still keep everyone else moving forward?

- Are there other strategies to help the learners who aren't getting it?

There is much for teams to consider before moving forward in any unit of instruction. The only time the decision to move forward can be based solely on numbers is when there is evidence that all learners are ready to move.

Motivation

Likewise, moving forward with learning involves activating motivation on behalf of the learner. Learners will choose not to engage if there is no possibility of future success. If the current structure of the assessment system is failing to motivate learners, teachers must take a step back and examine the overall system. In his work on motivation, researcher and author Daniel Pink (2010) states that the alternative to the traditional carrots and sticks as a means to motivate now includes new criteria: autonomy, mastery, and purpose.

- **Autonomy:** The learner is the number-one instructional decision maker in every classroom. He or she must gather meaningful information (not aggregate percentages or total points) following each assessment and then organize the data in a visible manner that shows a trajectory of growth throughout the duration of the unit of instruction. Ultimately, the learner must be able to make quality decisions about what comes next in his or her progression of learning, what skills and strategies he or she will bring to bear on the task ahead, and how he or she will monitor continued progress.

- **Mastery:** Formative assessments are used to build hope and foster efficacy. When formative assessments are managed well, the learner is able to make mistakes during the learning process and still demonstrate mastery by the end of the unit or learning period. In a rich formative assessment system, the learner can engage in error analysis: He or she gathers feedback and arranges his or her data and evidence in a manner that creates a clear view of patterns or anomalies in the data. At that point, he or she can then employ the strategies and skills necessary to create improvement in targeted and specific areas from one assessment to the next. He or she operates under the assurance that success is still possible. The summative assessment's resulting grades reflect an accurate score regarding the learner's mastery against a given set of standards and achievement-level descriptors, not an average of the sum total for all assessments during the unit.

- **Purpose:** The assessments tracked in data notebooks are engaging and meaningful. Literally, the learner can see worth in the data he or she is tracking. Most importantly, the culminating data enable the learner to draw healthy and accurate conclusions about his or her own self, developing insights into personal strengths and challenges and reflecting on favored content and learning styles. When the learning is provocative, engaging, and self-illuminating, the learner is better able to maintain a commitment to take risks and continue learning.

To reduce the game playing in second-chance testing, teachers must monitor the effectiveness of the system, making sure they do not reward those who get it right the first time with better grades than those who take multiple times to get it right. As tempting as this might be, it backfires in the end when the disengaged only become more disengaged because success is no longer possible. All learners must know that mastery is still possible and early mistakes will not be held against them. As early as kindergarten, learners will opt out of learning if they are clear that they have no chance to still be successful or obtain high marks.

Re-engagement

Learning is an unpredictable process. Instruction does not always go as planned, and some learners will require additional support and corrective responses (Chappuis, 2014; Wiliam, 2013). Some might reference this work as reteaching, but that suggests the work is on the learner's behalf.

When the instruction didn't work the first time, it is up to the teachers to find additional ways to re-engage the learners in new and interesting ways in order that they might learn. Re-engagement is an instructional process used to support learners who have struggled with one or more learning targets or expectations and have, as a result, failed to master the expectations at a level of proficiency. A balanced and productive formative assessment system should have prevented any learner from requiring wholesale reteaching of an entire unit of instruction. It is important for teachers to identify errors, misconceptions, and preconceived notions during the initial instruction so as to reduce the possibility that learners will require reteaching. Once it is discovered that some learners do require additional time and support, reteaching should be integrated into the instructional day, and it should not be punitive in tone (Buffum et al., 2012; DuFour, DuFour, & Eaker, 2008; DuFour et al., 2010).

A quality system for reteaching does not turn into ability grouping. It must truly involve flexible grouping. If it is discovered that the same learners are always qualifying for reteaching, then there is likely a system problem or a bias problem at play, and it must be examined and addressed immediately. *Who* requires intervention will vary from unit to unit, from learning target to learning target, and from error to error.

Imagine, for example, that a cadre of learners struggled to master the skill of inference. Figure 8.8 provides a description of the learning target and the possible errors that might result when learners struggle with inferring.

Learning Target: I can infer. This means when reading, I can make a good guess and support it with background knowledge and text clues.

Common Errors With Inference:

- The learner is being literal.
- The learner is making wild guesses.
- The learner is making a good guess but is only using background knowledge to support it.
- The learner is making a good guess but offers no details or clues to back it.

Figure 8.8: Error analysis with inference.

Teachers require quality diagnostic information to make informed instructional decisions, and these errors guide teachers in their decision making regarding next steps. The learner who is still being literal will benefit from a reteaching experience; however, the remaining learners will not require the reteaching of inference. A learner who is making wild guesses is likely struggling to understand text, and reteaching inference will not support his or her needs. Instead, that learner will likely benefit from word attack or decoding skills and comprehension strategies to support identifying main idea and details. The learners who are already making inferences should not be retaught how to infer; it would be a waste of precious time. Instead, those learners benefit from conducting their own error analysis or coaching and corrective feedback regarding their incomplete answers.

Once the strategy of reteaching is selected, then teachers must engage in thinking differently about the initial instruction. Many instructional models can work to support reteaching.

- Direct instruction presented in new or different ways
- Guided small-group work
- Targeted mini lessons based on a specific type of error or misconception
- Think-alouds
- Collaborative learning tasks (not peer teaching)
- Modeling
- Visual tools
- Manipulatives
- Computer-based courses, mini lessons, models
- Focused games or play
- Role plays

When teachers select an instructional model or strategy for re-engaging, they must keep the exact needs of the learners who will experience the learning in mind.

This, of course, does not mean that an intervention specialist or a special education specialist or a gifted education specialist could not step in to either provide the direct instruction or take part in planning the direct intervention with the classroom teachers. When it comes to mapping out interventions to target the needs of struggling learners, the *only* absolute involves treating the learners with the utmost respect and dignity (Kramer, 2015).

At this point in the learning journey, the learner—and quite possibly the teacher—has clearly demonstrated confusion, which can provide a "sweet spot" for learning (Andrade, 2013; Muller, 2008; Tomlinson & Moon, 2013; Wiliam, 2013). Productive struggle supports learning. Re-engaging, then, involves teacher and learner working together to more clearly and comprehensively diagnose the challenges that are blocking learning from occurring, and then providing the appropriate correction of responses. In this time and space, confusion can be leveraged as an instructional tool. It provides both teachers and students the opportunity to explore misconceptions, preconceived notions, and alternative pathways to understanding or mastering knowledge and skill (Chappuis, 2014; Moser, Schroder, Heeter, Moran, & Lee, 2011; Muller, 2008; Tomlinson & Moon, 2013).

Collaborative Common Assessments in Action: Reteaching for Mastery

Following a summative assessment, the teachers on a third-grade team realized they still had nine learners across the grade level who were struggling with the concept of inference. The team decided to pull the nine learners together during their language arts block for reteaching over the course of three days. The team created an interactive game of Clue in which each of the learners would adopt a role and then act the part with some small costume additions, if the learners desired to use them (but it was not required).

The team designed the entire project together, but only the teacher who had the best results with teaching inference during the unit of instruction would run the game in a reteaching experience for the struggling learners. The teacher running the game would serve as the lead detective in the mystery, but the names of all of the other third-grade teachers would be used as the suspects in the story, and one of them would be the actual culprit. In the scenario they created, the school's mascot and the jar of candy the mascot was holding were stolen from the principal's office. Each of the learners would play a role in helping to solve the mystery. The team created nine roles for the nine learners to fill: a police officer, three CSI agents, the school's principal, two of the third-grade teachers, the media specialist, and the school janitor.

The team wrote a series of clues that they would gradually release to the right players, and each player was given a clue that no one else could see with each new round of the game. With each clue a learner received, he or she was asked a question of inference at the bottom of the clue card. Each card provided space for the learners to write their answers to the clue-based question. For each answer the learner provided, he or she needed to add three specific clues or pieces of evidence that led him or her to believe the answer was accurate. At certain points in the game, the lead detective would call on one or more of the students and use the "5 Why" strategy (asking *why* five times in a row) to see if she could elicit more statements of inference from the learners.

Once the mystery was solved at the beginning of day two's lesson, the learners put all the cards with their answers and supporting evidence in the middle of the table. They began to sort their cards into groupings so they could look for patterns in their answers and discuss which answers best helped them solve the mystery. The teacher took note of their discoveries on the board.

Then, the learners were put into groups of three and asked to see if they could generate the same types of answers when reading a passage. They were given a short story and asked to work as a team to answer the inferential question, like CSI agents would. They had highlighters so they could highlight the clues that supported their answers. When they finished, they gathered as a large group to again compare answers and draw conclusions about their answers. At the end of day two, each learner was given an exit slip and asked to answer a different question of inference with an entirely different focus than the first question regarding the story they had just discussed. The third-grade team got together at the end of day two to explore the students' answers and identify trouble spots that the teacher running the reteaching unit would address on day three. Also on day three, the learners were provided with a short retest to see if the reteaching had been successful.

Error Analysis and Coaching

Not every learner requires a full explanation of the content, even if he or she has not yet mastered a targeted area on the summative assessment. Some learners simply need an opportunity to recognize the pattern that emerged in their errors, or the chance to practice to attain fluidity with the content, or the insight into additional strategies that can be used for addressing specific types of errors. The same "sorting cards by error" and "sorting cards by proficiency levels" activities that work well with helping teachers identify errors and collaboratively score work will support learners in their understanding as well. When teaching teams are done sorting cards and labeling types of mistakes or identifying proficiency levels, they can reach into the piles of cards and remove several that did not come from their own classrooms and that do not have student names anywhere on them. Teachers can then take those cards back into their classrooms and engage young learners in sorting cards, finding and labeling errors, scoring collaboratively, and problem solving collectively regarding next instructional steps for the work they see before them. Learners are better able to activate themselves or each other as instructional resources to address gaps in understanding or skill when they share a common picture of mastery with the instructional staff (Chappuis, 2014; Chappuis et al., 2012; Wiliam, 2013).

All learners—not just struggling learners—will likely need various moments of error analysis and coaching. It is just part of the learning journey, which often requires corrective feedback. Feedback is an instructional intervention. Teachers use it to help learners make instructional choices regarding how they can close their own gaps. It is a first line of defense when the going gets tough. Unfortunately, teachers rarely analyze student work to diagnose errors, misconceptions, or faulty reasoning (Schneider et al., 2013; Stiggins & Herrick, 2007; Wiliam,

2013). In a responsive delivery system, teachers work to gather valid, reliable, *and helpful* assessment data and artifacts that can help them improve their instructional responses. Even when engaged in initial instruction, feedback should only be used in situations in which there is something positive on which to build (Andrade, 2013; Chappuis, 2014; Hattie, 2009; Hattie & Timperley, 2007; Wiliam, 2013). Giving feedback before a foundation of understanding has been established can actually send the learner into further confusion. Hattie (2009) states:

> Feedback is information provided by an agent (e.g., teacher, peer, book, parent, or one's own experience) about aspects of one's performance or understanding. For example, a teacher or parent can provide corrective information, a peer can provide an alternative strategy, a book can provide information to clarify ideas, a parent can provide encouragement, and a learner can look up the answer to evaluate the correctness of a response. *Feedback is a "consequence" of performance.* (p. 174)

The purpose of feedback is to reduce discrepancies. Feedback must feed forward. Even in the coaching mode, feedback must be employed in appropriate ways. Andrade (2013) states:

> Feedback is most effective when it is the right kind (e.g. detailed and narrative, not graded), delivered in the right way (supportive), at the right time (sooner for low-level knowledge, but not so soon that it prevents metacognitive processing and later for complex tasks), and to the right person (who is in a receptive mood and has reasonably high self-efficacy). (p. 25)

All learners, no matter their initial results, require a sense of efficacy to move forward. Feedback can be used as an instructional activity as long as the learner has a foundation on which to build. Feedback offered without evidence that some degree of learning is already in place can be detrimental to a learner's success or ability to move forward (Chappuis, 2014; Hattie, 2009). Hattie (2009) notes that when feedback is combined with correctional review for instructional purposes, it must "provide information specifically relating to the task or process of learning that fills the gap between what is understood and what is aimed to be understood" (p. 174).

One part of the reteaching equation certainly involves including learners in the decision making and solution regarding their own learning. In an essay for the *New Yorker* titled "The Bell Curve," Atul Gawande (2004) provides a stunning example of Warren Warwick, a physician who partners with his cystic fibrosis patients as collaborative researchers regarding the most challenging circumstances in their medical care. Together, doctor and patient explore any and all available measures—sometimes designing altogether new alternatives—to address the patient's needs. Patients with cystic fibrosis survive longer under his care. Like a masterful teacher, Warwick seeks feedback from his patients. He involves them in creating solutions. And then he does not rest until he has understood the issues at hand and found new options to support those in his care. Master teachers engage in the same caliber of work, inviting their learners into diagnosing personal struggles and then co-creating solutions.

Far too often, the voice of the learner is left out of the critical decision making. Educators tend to make decisions about learners without including the learners. Very young students understand and can express, albeit sometimes with prompting, what helps them learn. Ask a kindergarten student what could have been better in the lesson, and be prepared for honesty! Hattie (2009) also finds that master teachers do not just *give* feedback; master teachers *seek* feedback, especially in challenging situations as a means to better understand how to support a struggling learner:

> It was only when I discovered that feedback was most powerful when it is from the *student to the teacher* that I started to understand it better. When teachers seek, or at least are open to, feedback from students as to what students know, what they understand, where they make errors, when they have misconceptions, when they are not engaged—then teaching and learning can be synchronized and powerful. Feedback to teachers helps make learning visible. (p. 173)

In this space, everyone—student and teacher alike—can become more informed and more accomplished. Such opportunities can provide magical moments. Reteaching should be embraced as an exciting opportunity rather than pure drudgery.

Collaborative Common Assessments in Action: Using Data to Differentiate Instruction and Intervention

The high school business management teacher, Mr. Weber, readily adopted the Speaking and Listening standards into his curriculum. During the actual unit on business presentations, Mr. Weber had helped his learners co-create a rubric for quality presentations; still, at the end of the unit, he noted he had a few learners in three sections of the class who were still struggling with various criteria on the rubric during their actual business presentations (three struggled with pacing, five struggled with eye contact, six struggled with responding to audience questions). Mr. Weber was confident that the learners understood the concepts involved and did not need to be retaught regarding those concepts. Instead, they needed coaching, focused practice with feedback, and opportunities to try again. He designed mini sessions for each small group based on the students' focus area, and he used the same process for each of the many sessions.

First, he put the learners together in a small group based on their area of need. Each group was asked to watch three different short videos of business presentations. The students were to work together using the rubric to come to consensus on what the score for their focus area (eye contact, responding to questions, and pacing) would be with each video clip. In addition, they needed to use specific evidence to back the scores they assigned. Mr. Weber took turns floating from one group to the next, listening in on the students' conversations, and asking exploratory questions that required them to dig more deeply into and then justify their own answers. The students in each group concluded their video session by working together to list the most common mistakes they found and then identify strategies they could use to avoid each type of mistake they found.

Following the guided discussion, each individual was charged with presenting another five-minute business presentation to a live audience outside of school (in his or her own home with family, in a park with friends, and then so on) and video recording the presentation, making sure his or her live audience was seen and heard asking questions that generated quality responses from the speaker.

Each learner was required to watch his or her own video, use the rubric to score the video, and then identify personal strengths and opportunities to grow based on the trait practiced. In addition, each learner was required to queue his or her video to the best one-minute segment of the overall performance. When ready, each learner scheduled a brief meeting with Mr. Weber. Patterned after the three-minute conference (Chappuis, 2014), the slightly longer four-minute feedback conference was set up in such a way that each minute served a specific purpose.

- **Minute 1:** Watch the one-minute segment that the learner selected together.
- **Minute 2:** The learner shared his or her self-generated rubric score as well as strengths and opportunities for growth regarding the focus area on the rubric.
- **Minute 3:** Mr. Weber added to the feedback, sharing his rubric score and ideas for strengths and opportunities for growth.
- **Minute 4:** Together, student and teacher discussed and designed next steps.

Finally, when Mr. Weber deemed each learner was ready, he or she was tasked with providing another presentation to the class, with the goal of demonstrating mastery in the desired trait.

Enrichment

Enrichment means that any or all aspects of the learning a learner experiences (curriculum, instruction, assessment, environment, and so on) will be enhanced or extended in a manner that re-engages the learner at an even higher level of application or critical thinking than was previously expected. When learners master the learning targets or standards in a unit of instruction, they can be engaged in enrichment as a means to deepen their learning, integrate concepts in meaningful and engaging ways, and simultaneously celebrate their achievements. Enrichment is not to be confused with any of the following:

- Adding more work

- Making harder problems

- Moving more quickly through the curriculum

- Making learners who mastered the content teach others who did not

- Engaging in something completely different from the learning targets studied

There are two significant reasons why the peer teaching model is less than ideal for enrichment, coaching, or reteaching opportunities: (1) learners who have demonstrated mastery should be granted the opportunity to truly extend and refine their own learning; and 2) learners who have struggled with their own learning require specific, diagnostic information and the attendant professional support to help them close gaps. While it is true that teaching something to someone else can deepen understanding, the learners who have already demonstrated understanding deserve the opportunity to extend their own learning. Learners who are ready for enrichment or extension experiences often resent needing to teach others the things that they themselves have already mastered. Moreover, the struggling learner has specific needs that should not be turned over to amateurs. Educators themselves can sometimes struggle with diagnosing gaps and errors accurately, and the learners in their care deserve the *best* possible support available.

Enrichment must truly extend the learners' knowledge, skills, and abilities regarding the current learning expectations in meaningful and exciting ways. Because learners have already demonstrated the levels of proficiency that qualified them to engage in an enrichment activity, it is not necessary for teachers to reassess students who qualify for enrichment. Learners engaged in enrichment activities typically generate products that can be used as evidence to monitor their continued growth over time.

In a collaborative common assessment system, the process for employing enrichments works best when the following conditions or circumstances are addressed:

- The team uses short cycle enrichments (not one long project over time, but shorter projects that tie directly to the learning targets of the unit of study) so that all learners have the opportunity to participate as they are able. This allows for flexible grouping rather than ability grouping. All learners should have the opportunity to experience enrichments.

- The teachers design the enrichment when they design the summative assessment—in advance of instruction—so the desired end results are clear and the image of *mastery* is understood throughout instruction.

- The learners are made aware of what the enrichment activity or activities will be if they master the learning targets in a timely fashion.

- The enrichment is designed in a manner that truly extends the learning opportunity regarding the exact targets studied during the unit. Moreover, the enrichment opportunity is provocative and challenging; learners would want to engage in the opportunity.

- The enrichment process is conducted at the same time that the coaching and reteaching processes are occurring. Such differentiation enables teachers to continue to deepen the learning while moving everyone forward in significant and targeted ways.

Because of the legislation that focuses educators' attention on interventions, because of the frequency of experiences, and because of the improving database on research-based instructional strategies, it is becoming clear that the work of planning and implementing intervention is actually easier to manage than enrichment. Systems like RTI have engaged teachers in better understanding interventions and monitoring student learning. But finding challenging, exciting, and worthy tasks or enrichment activities that truly extend the exact learning targets under review in meaningful ways can be challenging for teaching teams.

Enrichment and extension opportunities should be engaging and rewarding. They should create exciting and engaging learning opportunities that are accessible to all. They should not create a system of exclusivity that broadens the achievement gap; rather, enrichment opportunities should ignite curiosity, passion, creativity, fond memories, and proud moments for all.

Collaborative Common Assessments in Action: Enriching Learning

The fifth-grade team teachers decided to share their enrichment activity for the unit on measuring with fractions in advance of their initial instruction. They noticed an increase in motivation when learners discovered they could be part of the team that made the no-bake cookies during class time if they mastered their learning expectations by the time they were expected to take the summative assessment. The educators experienced the highest success rate with early completion of the standards. Only a handful of learners still required intervention services.

On the day of the enrichment activity, the teachers provided the learners with a cart full of ingredients, measuring tools, and a recipe filled with fractions. Teams were then tasked with increasing the recipe by 2.5. Now, learners would still be measuring with fractions, but this time they would be using fractions to increase the recipe already filled with fractions.

Encouraging Student Investment and Student Voice

When teachers make decisions regarding next instructional steps, they (hopefully) do so based on data generated from assessments. But there is another form of data that can be equally (if not more) powerful in the decision-making process—the learner's personal perspective regarding what is happening and what needs to happen with his or her own learning. Fortunately, more and more teams are using student self-reflection forms following an assessment so that the learner can personally identify strengths, opportunities for growth, next steps, and specific goals and action plans. But that is only one part of the equation, albeit an important part.

Educators would benefit from engaging in qualitative practices in which they seek feedback from the learners' perspectives. Learners have much to say regarding their own needs and desires for the educational system established to support them. Some of the learners' perspectives might not be easy for educators to hear; some of them might not even be welcome; yet, all of the qualitative feedback offered in the spirit of truly supporting their individual needs as learners can provide extremely meaningful growth opportunities for the educators that serve them. Like the learners they serve, educators must work on building hope and efficacy into their own self-regulated learning opportunities.

Collaborative Common Assessments in Action: Using Qualitative Feedback From Learners to Improve Programs

In the spring of each year, a high school engages in the practice of conducting focus groups with learners from grades 9 through 12. When forming the groups, staff members make sure to gather a truly random sample of learners from every grade level, ability level, grade point average, subject matter strength, and category of interests. When forming the questions for the focus groups, staff members make sure to link the questions to the specific school improvement goals of the past year. The focus group is conducted with the help of a moderator from the staff, and the entire staff of 250 members is expected to be in the audience to listen.

The moderator always begins the one-hour focus group conversation by establishing the ground rules for the conversation that will create safety for students and teachers alike. The rules include things like the following:

- Everything you say here will remain confidential. Your comments will not be held against you outside of this room. The teachers will not address your comments with you personally; likewise, the teachers invite you to discuss your comments following this hour-long conversation. This is meant to protect you from any potential rebuttals following our time together.

- Please refrain from using individual teachers' names in your comments. Speak generally about your overall educational experience in our school.

- Try to offer constructive feedback that will help us better serve you.

- Please refrain from inappropriate references or language. This is a professional learning opportunity for everyone involved. We must all be on our best conduct.

The year the high school launched a focused effort to improve educational equity, the staff asked learners specific questions about their instruction and assessment practices related to supporting diversity for the learners. The moderator of the panel noted that a petite English learner, a junior in the high school, opted not to speak throughout the entire focus group, even when encouraged to do so. The moderator decided it would be safer for the learner if she were not forced to participate. Everyone, including the moderator, was surprised at the end of the conversation when suddenly the young woman stood and began to speak in broken English. With tears in her eyes and a quiver in her voice, she said, "I no speak English. Because I no speak English, teachers think me dumb, so they won't ask me the questions." She paused, and then added with emphasis on each individual word, "I *want* to answer the questions!"

Student voice is a powerful and untapped data source in the intervention process. It is like an energy source that has always existed but has not yet been activated. When teachers and learners work together, they can isolate the individual's *learning DNA* (desires, needs, and assets). Such data are invaluable in the teaching and learning process.

Expecting Career and College Readiness—All Learners, All the Time

Education is serious business. It can certainly be as life-threatening as the medical profession might be. There is an expression that rings true: *What you think of me, I'll think of me; what I think of me, I'll be.* Educators make or break career pathways—entire life choices—for young learners. Expectations must remain high, and educational opportunities must remain focused and plentiful if educators are to achieve the goal of all learners being career and college ready. Kendall (2011) states:

> Education is a complex and challenging enterprise. Within K–12 education are found the hopes of parents, the promise of children, and, ultimately, the future of a society. The challenges are as significant as the consequences for failure. We do know a few things. We know that the teacher has the single greatest influence on student learning in the school, and that the backgrounds and experiences students bring to the classroom have an enormous effect on the degree to which those students flourish or struggle to succeed. We also know that holding students to high standards drives them to work to meet what is expected of them. (pp. 55–56)

To accomplish this enormous task, educators must work collaboratively. They must explore their own results deeply and commit to improving their practice. They must set ego aside and place the needs of the learners first. As Larry I. Bell (2002/2003) reminds educators, "As long as you are a teacher, even on your worst day on the job, you are still some student's best hope" (p. 34). Committing to collaboratively improving assessment and instruction practices is committing to learners and their hope for the future.

References and Resources

Ainsworth, L. (2003). *Power standards: Identifying the standards that matter the most*. Englewood, CO: Advanced Learning Press.

Ainsworth, L., & Viegut, D. (2006). *Common formative assessments: How to connect standards-based instruction and assessment*. Thousand Oaks, CA: Corwin Press.

Almeida, L. (2007). The journey toward effective assessment for English language learners. In D. Reeves (Ed.), *Ahead of the curve: The power of assessment to transform teaching and learning* (pp. 147–163). Bloomington, IN: Solution Tree Press.

Almond, P., Winter, P., Cameto, R., Russell, M., Sato, E., Clarke-Midura, J., et al. (2010). *Technology-enabled and universally designed assessment: Considering access in measuring the achievement of students with disabilities—A foundation for research*. Dover, NH: Measured Progress.

Anderson, L. W., & Krathwohl, D. R. (Eds.). (2001). *A taxonomy for learning, teaching, and assessing: A revision of Bloom's taxonomy of educational objectives* (Complete ed.). New York: Longman.

Andrade, H. L. (2013). Classroom assessment in the context of learning theory and research. In J. H. McMillan (Ed.), *SAGE handbook of research on classroom assessment* (pp. 17–34). Thousand Oaks, CA: SAGE.

Bailey, K., & Jakicic, C. (2012). *Common formative assessment: A toolkit for Professional Learning Communities at Work*. Bloomington, IN: Solution Tree Press.

Bandura, A. (1977). Self-efficacy: Toward a unifying theory of behavioral change. *Psychological Review, 34*(2), 191–215.

Bandura, A. (1997). *Self-efficacy: The exercise of control*. New York: Freeman.

Bandura, A. (2006). Adolescent development from an agentic perspective. In F. Pajares & T. Urdan (Eds.), *Self-efficacy beliefs of adolescents* (pp. 1–43). Greenwich, CT: Information Age.

Bell, L. I. (2002/2003). Strategies that close the gap. *Educational Leadership, 60*(4), 32–34.

Black, P., Harrison, C., Lee, C., Marshall, B., & Wiliam, D. (2004). Working inside the black box: Assessment for learning in the classroom. *Phi Delta Kappan, 86*(1), 9–21.

Black, P., & Wiliam, D. (1998). Inside the black box: Raising standards through classroom assessment. *Phi Delta Kappan, 80*(2), 139–148.

Blanchard, K. (2007). *Leading at a higher level: Blanchard on leadership and creating high performing organizations.* Upper Saddle River, NJ: Prentice Hall.

Bloom, B. S. (Ed.) (1956). *Taxonomy of educational objectives, book I: Cognitive domain.* New York: McKay.

Brinson, D., & Steiner, L. (2007, October). *Building collective efficacy: How leaders inspire teachers to achieve* (Issue Brief). Washington, DC: Center for Comprehensive School Reform and Improvement.

Brown, B. (2010). *The gifts of imperfection: Let go of who you think you're supposed to be and embrace who you are.* Center City, MN: Hazelden.

Buffum, A., Mattos, M., & Weber, C. (2012). *Simplifying response to intervention: Four essential guiding principles.* Bloomington, IN: Solution Tree Press.

Calkins, L., Ehrenworth, M., & Lehman, C. (2012). *Pathways to the Common Core: Accelerating achievement.* Portsmouth, NH: Heinemann.

Catmull, E., & Wallace, A. (2014). *Creativity, Inc.: Overcoming the unseen forces that stand in the way of true inspiration.* New York: Random House.

Chappuis, J. (2009). *Seven strategies of assessment for learning.* Portland, OR: Pearson Assessment Training Institute.

Chappuis, J. (2014). *Seven strategies of assessment for learning* (2nd ed.). Portland, OR: Pearson Assessment Training Institute.

Chappuis, J., Stiggins, R., Chappuis, S., & Arter, J. (2012). *Classroom assessment for student learning: Doing it right—using it well* (2nd ed.). Upper Saddle River, NJ: Pearson Education.

Chappuis, S., Chappuis, J., & Stiggins, R. (2009). Suporting teacher learning teams. *Educational Leadership, 66*(5), 56–60.

Chenoweth, K. (2007). *It's being done: Academic success in unexpected schools.* Cambridge, MA: Harvard Education Press.

Chenoweth, K. (2009a). *How it's being done: Urgent lessons from unexpected schools.* Cambridge, MA: Harvard Education Press.

Chenoweth, K. (2009b). It can be done, it's being done, and here's how. *Phi Delta Kappan, 91*(1), 38–43.

Chenoweth, K., & Theokas, C. (2011). *Getting it done: Leading academic success in unexpected schools.* Cambridge, MA: Harvard Education Press.

Clarke, S. (2001). *Unlocking formative assessment: Practical strategies for enhancing pupils' learning in the primary classroom.* London: Hodder Education.

Clarke, S. (2005). *Formative assessment in action: Weaving the elements together.* London: Hodder Education.

Clarke, S. (2008). *Active learning through formative assessment.* London: Hodder Education.

Conzemius, A., & O'Neill, J. (2014). *The handbook for SMART school teams: Revitalizing best practices for collaboration* (2nd ed.). Bloomington, IN: Solution Tree Press.

Corcoran, S. P. (2010). *Can teachers be evaluated by their students' test scores? Should they be? The use of value-added measures of teacher effectiveness in policy and practice* (Education Policy for Action Series). Providence, RI: Annenberg Institute for School Reform at Brown University.

Costa, A. L. (2008). *The school as a home for the mind: Creating mindful curriculum, instruction, and dialogue.* Thousand Oaks, CA: Corwin Press.

Csikszentmihalyi, M. (2009). *Creativity: Flow and the psychology of discovery and invention.* New York: HarperCollins.

Daggett, W. R. (2008). *Achieving academic excellence through rigor and relevance.* Rexford, NY: International Center for Leadership in Education. Accessed at www.leadered.com/pdf /Achieving_Academic_Excellence_2014.pdf on April 7, 2011.

Davies, A. (2011). *Making classroom assessment work* (3rd ed.). Courtenay, British Columbia, Canada: Connections.

D'Mello, S., Lehman, B., Pekrun, R., & Graesser, A. (2014). Confusion can be beneficial for learning. *Learning and Instruction, 29*(1), 153–170.

Dolan, R. P., & Hall, T. E. (2001). Universal design for learning: Implications for large-scale assessment. *IDA Perspectives, 27*(4), 22–25.

DuFour, R., DuFour, R., & Eaker, R. (2008). *Revisiting Professional Learning Communities at Work: New insights for improving schools.* Bloomington, IN: Solution Tree Press.

DuFour, R., DuFour, R., Eaker, R., & Many, T. (2006). *Learning by doing: A handbook for Professional Learning Communities at Work.* Bloomington, IN: Solution Tree Press.

DuFour, R., DuFour, R., Eaker, R., & Many, T. (2010). *Learning by doing: A handbook for Professional Learning Communities at Work* (2nd ed.). Bloomington, IN: Solution Tree Press.

DuFour, R., & Fullan, M. (2013). *Cultures built to last: Systemic PLCs at Work.* Bloomington, IN: Solution Tree Press.

DuFour, R., & Marzano, R. J. (2011). *Leaders of learning: How district, school, and classroom leaders improve student achievement.* Bloomington, IN: Solution Tree Press.

DuFour, R., & Mattos, M. (2013). How do principals really improve schools? *Educational Leadership, 70*(7), 34–40.

Elmore, R. (2004). *School reform from the inside out: Policy, practice, and performance.* Cambridge, MA: Harvard Education Press.

Engle, R. A. (2012). The resurgence of research into transfer: An introduction to the final articles of the transfer strand. *Journal of the Learning Sciences, 21*(3), 347–352.

Erkens, C. (2009). Developing our assessment literacy. In T. R. Guskey (Ed.), *The teacher as assessment leader* (pp. 11–30). Bloomington, IN: Solution Tree Press.

Erkens, C. (2016). *The handbook for collaborative common assessments: Tools for design, delivery, and data analysis.* Bloomington, IN: Solution Tree Press.

Erkens, C., & Twadell, E. (2012). *Leading by design: An action framework for PLC at Work leaders.* Bloomington, IN: Solution Tree Press.

Fisher, D., & Frey, N. (2007). *Checking for understanding: Formative assessment techniques for your classroom.* Alexandria, VA: Association for Supervision and Curriculum Development.

Fisher, D., & Frey, N. (2012). Making time for feedback. *Educational Leadership, 70*(1), 42–46.

Fullan, M. (2008). *The six secrets of change: What the best leaders do to help their organizations survive and thrive.* San Francisco: Jossey-Bass.

Fullan, M. (2011). *The moral imperative realized.* Thousand Oaks, CA: Corwin Press.

Fullan, M., Bertani, A., & Quinn, J. (2004). New lessons for districtwide reform. *Educational Leadership, 61*(7), 42–46.

Gallimore, R., Ermeling, B. A., Saunders, W. M., & Goldenberg, C. (2009). Moving the learning of teaching closer to practice: Teacher education implications of school-based inquiry teams. *Elementary School Journal, 109*(5), 537–551.

Gawande, A. (2004, December 6). The bell curve. *New Yorker.* Accessed at www.newyorker .com/archive/2004/12/06/041206fa_fact on June 28, 2014.

Goddard, R. D., Hoy, W. K., & Hoy, A. W. (2000). Collective teacher efficacy: Its meaning, measure, and impact on student achievement. *American Educational Research Journal, 37*(2), 479–507.

Goddard, R. D., & Skrla, L. (2006). The influence of school social composition on teachers' collective efficacy beliefs. *Educational Administration Quarterly, 42*(2), 216–235.

Goertz, M. E., Oláh, L. N., & Riggan, M. (2009, December). From testing to teaching: The use of interim assessments in classroom instruction (CPRE Research Report #RR-65). Philadelphia: Consortium for Policy Research in Education.

Hargreaves, E. (2007). The validity of collaborative assessment for learning. *Assessment in Education: Principles, Policy and Practice, 14*(2), 185–199.

Hattie, J. (2009). *Visible learning: A synthesis of over 800 meta-analyses relating to achievement.* New York: Routledge.

Hattie, J. (2012). *Visible learning for teachers: Maximizing impact on learning.* New York: Routledge.

Hattie, J., & Timperley, H. (2007). The power of feedback. *Review of Educational Research, 77*(1), 81–112.

Heritage, M. (2010). *Formative assessment: Making it happen in the classroom.* Thousand Oaks, CA: Corwin Press.

Heritage, M. (2013). Gathering evidence of student understanding. In J. H. McMillan (Ed.), *SAGE handbook of research on classroom assessment* (pp. 179–196). Thousand Oaks, CA: SAGE.

Hess, K. K., Carlock, D., Jones, B., & Walkup, J. R. (2010, June). *What exactly do "fewer, clearer, and higher standards" really look like in the classroom? Using a cognitive rigor matrix to analyze curriculum, plan lessons, and implement assessments.* Presentation at the Council of Chief State School Officers National Conference, Detroit, MI. Accessed at http://schools.nyc.gov/NR /rdonlyres/D106125F-FFF0420E-86D9254761638C6F/0/HessArticle.pdf on August 30, 2014.

Hockett, J. A., & Doubet, K. J. (2013/2014). Turning on the lights: What pre-assessments can do. *Educational Leadership, 71*(4), 50–54.

Hoy, W. K., Sweetland, S. R., & Smith, P. A. (2002). Toward an organizational model of achievement in high schools: The significance of collective efficacy. *Educational Administration Quarterly, 38*(1), 77–93.

Jacobs, H. H. (1997). *Mapping the big picture: Integrating curriculum and assessment K–12.* Alexandria, VA: Association for Supervision and Curriculum Development.

Kendall, J. (2011). *Understanding Common Core State Standards.* Alexandria, VA: Association for Supervision and Curriculum Development.

Kramer, S. V. (2015). Choosing prevention before intervention. In A. Buffum & M. Mattos (Eds.), *It's about time: Planning interventions and extensions in elementary school* (pp. 15–29). Bloomington, IN: Solution Tree Press.

Lencioni, P. (2005). *Overcoming the five dysfunctions of a team: A field guide for leaders, managers, and facilitators.* San Francisco: Jossey-Bass.

Marshall, K. (2008). Interim assessments: A user's guide. *Phi Delta Kappan, 90*(1), 64–68.

Marzano, R. J. (2003). *What works in schools: Translating research into action.* Alexandria, VA: Association for Supervision and Curriculum Development.

Marzano, R. J. (2006). *Classroom assessment & grading that work.* Alexandria, VA: Association for Supervision and Curriculum Development.

Marzano, R. J. (2007). *The art and science of teaching: A comprehensive framework for effective instruction.* Alexandria, VA: Association for Supervision and Curriculum Development.

Marzano, R. J., & Kendall, J. S. (2007). *The new taxonomy of educational objectives* (2nd ed.). Thousand Oaks, CA: Corwin Press.

McMillan, J. H. (Ed.). (2013a). *SAGE handbook of research on classroom assessment.* Thousand Oaks, CA: SAGE.

McMillan, J. H. (2013b). Why we need research on classroom assessment. In J. H. McMillan (Ed.), *SAGE handbook of research on classroom assessment* (pp. 3–16). Thousand Oaks, CA: SAGE.

McTighe, J., & Ferrara, S. (2000). *Assessing learning in the classroom.* Washington, DC: National Education Association.

Meisels, S. J., Atkins-Burnett, S., Xue, Y., Bickel, D. D., Son, S.-H., & Nicholson, J. (2003). Creating a system of accountability: The impact of instructional assessment on elementary children's achievement test scores. *Educational Policy Analysis Archives, 11*(9), 19. Accessed at http://epaa.asu
.edu/eapp/v11n9 on February 12, 2015.

Meyer, D. (2010, March). *Math class needs a makeover* [Video file]. Accessed at www.ted.com/talks
/dan_meyer_math_curriculum_makeover on February 12, 2015.

Moser, J. S., Schroder, H. S., Heeter, C., Moran, T. P., & Lee, Y.-H. (2011). Mind your errors: Evidence for a neural mechanism linking growth mind-set to adaptive posterror adjustments. *Psychological Science, 22*(12), 1484–1489.

Moss, C. M., & Brookhart, S. M. (2012). *Learning targets: Helping students aim for understanding in today's lesson.* Alexandria, VA: Association for Supervision and Curriculum Development.

Muller, D. A. (2008). *Designing effective multimedia for physics education* (Unpublished doctoral thesis). School of Physics, University of Sydney, Australia. Accessed at www.physics.usyd.edu
.au/super/theses/PhD%28Muller%29.pdf on February 12, 2015.

National Council for the Social Studies. (2013). *College, career and civic life (C3) framework for social studies state standards: Guidance for enhancing the rigor of K–12 civics, economics, geography, and history.* Silver Spring, MD: Author.

National Education Association. (n.d.). *Preparing 21st century students for a global society: An educator's guide to the "Four Cs."* Accessed at www.nea.org/assets/docs/A-Guide-to-Four-Cs.pdf on March 14, 2014.

National Governors Association Center for Best Practices & Council of Chief State School Officers. (2010a). *Common Core State Standards for English language arts and literacy in history/social studies, science, and technical subjects.* Washington, DC: Authors. Accessed at www.corestandards.org/assets/CCSSI_ELA%20Standards.pdf on November 4, 2015.

National Governors Association Center for Best Practices & Council of Chief State School Officers. (2010b). *Common Core State Standards for mathematics.* Washington, DC: Authors. Accessed at www.corestandards.org/assets/CCSSI_Math%20Standards.pdf on November 4, 2015.

Newmann, F. M., King, M. B., & Carmichael, D. L. (2007). *Authentic instruction and assessment: Common standards for rigor and relevance in teaching academic subjects.* Des Moines, IA: Iowa Department of Education.

Odden, A. R., & Archibald, S. J. (2009). *Doubling student performance . . . and finding the resources to do it.* Thousand Oaks, CA: Corwin Press.

Ogle, R. (2007). *Smart world: Breakthrough creativity and the new science of ideas.* Boston: Harvard Business School Press.

"Oliver Wendell Holmes Sr." (2015). Accessed at http://famousquotesfrom.com/oliver-wendell-holmes-sr on November 8, 2015.

Organisation for Economic Co-operation and Development. (2011). *Strong performers and successful reformers in education: Lessons from PISA for the United States.* Paris: Author. Accessed at http://dx.doi.org/10.1787/9789264096660-en on February 12, 2015.

Patterson, K., Grenny, J., Maxfield, D., McMillan, R., & Switzler, A. (2008). *Influencer: The power to change anything.* New York: McGraw-Hill.

Pfeffer, J., & Sutton, R. I. (2006). *Hard facts, dangerous half-truths and total nonsense: Profiting from evidence-based management.* Boston: Harvard Business School Press.

Pink, D. H. (2005). *A whole new mind: Moving from the information age to the conceptual age.* New York: Riverhead Books.

Pink, D. H. (2010). *Drive: The surprising truth about what motivates us.* New York: Riverhead Books.

Popham, W. J. (2012a). Appropriate and inappropriate tests for evaluating schools [Pamphlet 1]. In *Mastering assessment: A self-service system for educators* (2nd ed.). Boston: Pearson Education.

Popham, W. J. (2012b). Assessment bias: How to banish it [Pamphlet 4]. In *Mastering assessment: A self-service system for educators* (2nd ed.). Boston: Pearson Education.

Popham, W. J. (2012c). Reliability: What is it and is it necessary? [Pamphlet 11]. In *Mastering assessment: A self-service system for educators* (2nd ed.). Boston: Pearson Education.

Protheroe, N. (2008). Teacher efficacy: What is it and does it matter? *Principal, 87*(5), 42–45.

Reeves, D. (Ed.). (2007). *Ahead of the curve: The power of assessment to transform teaching and learning.* Bloomington, IN: Solution Tree Press.

Reeves, D. B. (2002). *The leader's guide to standards: A blueprint for educational equity and excellence.* San Francisco: Jossey-Bass.

Reeves, D. B. (2004). *Accountability for learning: How teachers and school leaders can take charge.* Alexandria, VA: Association for Supervision and Curriculum Development.

Reeves, D. B. (2005). *Accountability in action: A blueprint for learning organizations* (2nd ed.). Englewood, CO: Advanced Learning Press.

Reeves, D. B. (2006). *The learning leader: How to focus school improvement for better results.* Alexandria, VA: Association for Supervision and Curriculum Development.

Resnick, L. B., & Berger, L. (2010). *An American examination system.* Austin, TX: National Conference on Next Generation Assessment Systems. Accessed at www.k12center.org /rsc/pdf/ResnickBergerSystemModel.pdf on May 30, 2014.

Ripley, A. (2013). *The smartest kids in the world: And how they got that way.* New York: Simon & Schuster.

Robinson, K. (2013). *Finding your element: How to discover your talents and passions and transform your life.* New York: Viking.

Rodriguez, M. C. (2004). The role of classroom assessment in student performance on TIMSS. *Applied Measurement in Education, 17*(1), 1–24.

Rodriguez, M. C., & Haladyna, T. M. (2013). Writing selected-response items for classroom assessment. In J. H. McMillan (Ed.), *SAGE handbook of research on classroom assessment* (pp. 293–311). Thousand Oaks, CA: SAGE.

Ross, J. A., & Gray, P. (2006). Transformational leadership and teacher commitment to organizational values: The mediating effects of collective teacher efficacy. *School Effectiveness and School Improvement, 17*(2), 179–199.

Ruiz-Primo, M. A., & Li, M. (2011). *Looking into teachers' feedback practices: How teachers interpret students' work.* Paper presented at the annual meeting of the American Educational Research Association, New Orleans, LA.

Schmoker, M. (2011). *Focus: Elevating the essentials to radically improve student learning.* Alexandria, VA: Association for Supervision and Curriculum Development.

Schneider, C., & Gowan, P. (2011). *Deconstructing student work: Investigating teachers' abilities to use evidence of student learning to inform instruction.* Paper presented at the annual meeting of the American Educational Research Association, New Orleans, LA.

Schneider, M. C., Egan, K. L., & Julian, M. W. (2013). Classroom assessment in the context of high-stakes testing. In J. H. McMillan (Ed.), *SAGE handbook of research on classroom assessment* (pp. 55–70). Thousand Oaks, CA: SAGE.

Scobie-Jennings, E. (n.d.). *"Josh could do better": Bringing out the best in underachieving gifted and talented students.* Accessed at www.academia.edu/4714396/Josh_could_do_better_Bringing _out_the_best_in_Underachieving_Gifted_and_Talented_Students on February 12, 2015.

Senge, P. M. (2006). *The fifth discipline: The art and practice of the learning organization* (Rev. ed.). New York: Doubleday.

Sergiovanni, T. J. (1992). *Moral leadership: Getting to the heart of school improvement.* San Francisco: Jossey-Bass.

Shaughnessy, M. F. (2004). An interview with Anita Woolfolk: The educational psychology of teacher efficacy. *Educational Psychology Review, 16*(2), 153–175.

Shepard, L. A. (2013). Foreword. In J. H. McMillan (Ed.), *SAGE handbook of research on classroom assessment* (pp. xix–xxv). Thousand Oaks, CA: SAGE.

Shim, H. S., & Roth, G. L. (2008). Sharing tacit knowledge among expert teaching professors and mentees: Considerations for career and technical education teacher educators. *Journal of Industrial Teacher Education, 44*(4), 5–28.

Stefanakis, E. H. (2002). *Multiple intelligences and portfolios: A window into the learner's mind.* Portsmouth, NH: Heinemann.

Stiggins, R. J. (2001). *Student-involved classroom assessment* (3rd ed.). Upper Saddle River, NJ: Merrill Prentice Hall.

Stiggins, R. J. (2007). Five assessment myths and their consequences [Commentary]. *Education Week, 27*(8), 28–29.

Stiggins, R. J. (2008, April). *Assessment manifesto: A call for the development of balanced assessment systems.* Portland, OR: ETS Assessment Training Institute.

Stiggins, R. J., & Chappuis, J. (2005). Using student-involved classroom assessment to close achievement gaps. *Theory Into Practice, 44*(1), 11–18.

Stiggins, R. J., & Herrick, M. (2007). *A status report on teacher preparation in classroom assessment.* Unpublished manuscript.

Strong, R. W., Silver, H. F., & Perini, M. J. (2001). *Teaching what matters most: Standards and strategies for raising student achievement.* Alexandria, VA: Association for Supervision and Curriculum Development.

Supovitz, J. A., & Christman, J. B. (2003, November). *Developing communities of instructional practice: Lessons from Cincinnati and Philadelphia* (CPRE Policy Brief RB-39). Philadelphia: Consortium for Policy Research in Education.

Talbert, J. E. (2010). Professional learning communities at the crossroads: How systems hinder or engender change. In A. Hargreaves, A. Lieberman, M. Fullan, & D. Hopkins (Eds.), *Second international handbook of educational change* (Vol. 23, pp. 555–571). London: Springer.

Thompson, S. J., Johnstone, C. J., & Thurlow, M. L. (2002). *Universal design applied to large scale assessments* (NCEO Synthesis Report 44). Minneapolis, MN: National Center on Educational Outcomes. Accessed at http://education.umn.edu/NCEO/OnlinePubs /Synthesis44.html on February 12, 2015.

Timperley, H. (2009). *Using assessment data for improving teaching practice.* Accessed at http://research.acer.edu.au/cgi/viewcontent.cgi?article=1036&context=research_conference on April 3, 2012.

Tomlinson, C. A. (2013/2014). One to grow on: Let's not dilute mastery. *Educational Leadership, 71*(4), 88–89.

Tomlinson, C. A., & Moon, T. R. (2013). Differentiation and classroom assessment. In J. H. McMillan (Ed.), *SAGE handbook of research on classroom assessment* (pp. 415–430). Thousand Oaks, CA: SAGE.

Torrance, H., & Pryor, J. (2001). Developing formative assessment in the classroom: Using action research to explore and modify theory. *British Educational Research Journal, 27*(5), 615–631.

Umphrey, J. (2008). Producing learning: A conversation with Robert Marzano. *Principal Leadership, 8*(5), 16–20.

Vagle, N. D. (2015). *Design in five: Essential phases to create engaging assessment practice.* Bloomington, IN: Solution Tree Press.

Wagner, T. (2008). Rigor redefined. *Educational Leadership, 66*(2), 20–25.

Webb, N. L. (2002). *Depth-of-knowledge levels for four content areas.* Unpublished manuscript. Accessed at www.hed.state.nm.us/uploads/files/ABE/Policies/depth_of_knowledge_guide _for_all_subject_areas.pdf on August 30, 2014.

Webb, N. L., Alt, M., Ely, R., & Vesperman, B. (2005, July). *Web alignment tool (WAT) training manual.* Madison, WI: Wisconsin Center for Education Research.

Weigle, S. C. (2007). Teaching writing teachers about assessment. *Journal of Second Language Writing, 16*(3), 194–209.

Wiggins, G. P., & McTighe, J. (1998). *Understanding by design.* Alexandria, VA: Association for Supervision and Curriculum Development.

Wiggins, G. P., & McTighe, J. (2007). *Schooling by design: Mission, action, and achievement.* Alexandria, VA: Association for Supervision and Curriculum Development.

Wiliam, D. (1998, July). *The validity of teachers' assessments.* Paper presented to Working Group 6 of the 22nd annual conference of the International Group for the Psychology of Mathematics Education, Stellenbosch, South Africa.

Wiliam, D. (2001). Reliability, validity, and all that jazz. *Education 3–13: International Journal of Primary, Elementary and Early Years Education, 29*(3), 17–21.

Wiliam, D. (2009, May 7). *The reliability of educational assessments.* Presentation slides from the Ofqual Annual Lecture, Coventry, West Midlands, England. Accessed at www.google.com /url?sa=t&rct=j&q=&esrc=s&source=web&cd=3&ved=0CDMQFjAC&url=http% 3A%2F%2Fwww.dylanwiliam.org%2FDylan_Wiliams_website%2FPresentations_ files%2FOfqual%2520talk.ppt&ei=hC8CVKCWO4GtyATfi4CwAw&usg=AFQjCNEY9BB MxWdk4H0d4rCBGFMUBsMCeA&sig2=1qALV04JYUCNECp5cwp9zw&bvm=bv.74115 972,d.aWw on August 30, 2014.

Wiliam, D. (2011). *Embedded formative assessment.* Bloomington, IN: Solution Tree Press.

Wiliam, D. (2013). Feedback and instructional correctives. In J. H. McMillan (Ed.), *SAGE handbook of research on classroom assessment* (pp. 197–214). Thousand Oaks, CA: SAGE.

Wiliam, D., & Thompson, M. (2007). Integrating assessment with learning: What will it take to make it work? In C. A. Dwyer (Ed.), *The future of assessment: Shaping, teaching, and learning* (pp. 53–84). Mahwah, NJ: Erlbaum.

Wright, R. J. (2008). *Educational assessment: Tests and measurements in the age of accountability.* Thousand Oaks, CA: SAGE.

Xu, Y. (2013). Classroom assessment in special education. In J. H. McMillan (Ed.), *SAGE handbook of research on classroom assessment* (pp. 431–447). Thousand Oaks, CA: SAGE.

Index

A

action research, 101–103
Ainsworth, L., 58
Almeida, L., 53
Andrade, H., 123, 133, 150
Arter, J., 61
assessments
    See also collaborative common assessments
    architects of, 17–19
    classroom, 31–33
    cohort-referenced, 22–23
    criterion-referenced, 22
    difference between evaluation and, 89
    formative, 85–88, 90–92
    high-stakes, 23–24
    improving, 132–135
    interim (benchmark, progress monitoring), 24–28
    large-scale (end-of-year), 21–22
    literacy, 84
    maps/plans, 65–68
    modified, 52
    norm-referenced, 22–23
    pre-, 93–94
    problem with, 1–3
    redefining, 89–92
    shallow, 22
    summative, 89–90, 91
    support between, 142–143
    system of, 19–28
    team, 28–31
autonomy, 144–145

B

Bell, A. G., 55
Bell, L. I., 157
Black, P., 92
Bloom's Revised Taxonomy, 79
Buffum, A., 51

C

Catmull, E., 14
Center for Equity and Excellence in Education, 52
Chappuis, J., 61
Chappuis, S., 61
Clarke, S., 61
classroom assessments, 31–33
coaching, 143, 149–151
cognitive complexity frameworks, 79
cohort-referenced assessments, 22–23
collaborative common assessments
    See also assessments
    corollary questions, 30–31
    defined, 6–7
    foundation for, 9
    methods, 81–83
    process, 7–14
    role of, 14–15
collaborative work/purpose
    cross-district teamwork, 47–48
    empowering teams, 131–132
    horizontal alignment, 42–47
    modified assessments,
    singletons, plus one, 49–50
    standards, 35–36

students with special needs, 50–54

    universal design,

    vertical alignment, 40–42

    whole school, 37–40

constructed response, 81, 82

criterion-referenced assessments, 22

cross-district teamwork, 47–48

curriculum, improving, 129–130

D

data phase

    artifacts, mining, 116–117

    conversations, 106–117

    description of, 12–13

    errors, analyzing types of, 118–121

    evidence to prove or disprove data, 114–115

    learning target needs and the use of error analysis, 121–126

    learning targets, diagnosing, 107–114

    obtaining common data, 115–116

    protocol, 106–107

delivery phase

    action research, 101–103

    assessment, redefining, 89–92

    assessments within instruction, 92–101

    components of, 86

    description of, 11–12

    formative assessments/context, 85–88, 90–92

    frequent formatives, 95–98

    integrated interventions, 98–101

    preassessments, 93–94

    pretests and post-tests, 93–95

    summative assessment, 89–90, 91

design phase

    benefits of, 71

    components of, 72

    creating and revising assessments, 76–77

    creation of individual assessments, 78–80

    delegation and division of parts and sections, 75–76

    description of, 9–10

    guidelines, 80–81

        predeveloped assessments, using, 74–75

        protocols for, 73–80

differentiation, 94, 137–140, 151–152

Doubet, K., 93

DuFour, R., 6, 29–30, 50, 137

E

Eaker, R., 6, 29–30, 50, 137

effective teaching, 87

Egan, K., 19, 91, 118

Einstein, A., 140

end-of-year (large-scale) assessments, 21–22

English learners, 51, 52, 53

enrichment, 153–155

Erkens, C., 4, 59, 60, 74, 107, 114, 116

errors, analyzing types of, 118–121

essential learning (priority standards), identifying, 56–60

evaluation, difference between assessment and, 89

F

feedback, 150–151, 155–156

Fisher, D., 119

flash meetings, 97

formative assessments, 85–88, 90–92

frequent formatives, 95–98

Frey, N., 119

G

Gawande, A., 150

goals, establishing SMART, 63–65

H

Handbook for Collaborative Common Assessments, The (Erkens), 4, 59, 60, 74, 84, 107, 112, 114, 116, 120

Hattie, J., 150, 151

Herrick, M., 32

high-stakes assessments, 23–24

Hockett, J., 93

Holmes, O. W., Sr., 130

horizontal alignment, 42–47

I

Individuals with Disabilities Education Act (IDEA), 51–52

instruction, improving, 130–131

interim (benchmark, progress monitoring) assessments, 24–28

interventions, integrated, 98–101

J

Jobs, S., 71

Julian, M., 19, 91, 118

K

Keller, H., 35

Kendall, J., 157

Kouzes, J., 5

Kramer, S., 135, 139

L

large-scale assessments (end-of-year), 21–22

learning, when to advance, 144–145

learning culture, 91–92

learning targets

    defining, 60–62

    diagnosing, 107–114

    needs and the use of error analysis, 121–126

Lombardi, V., 1

M

Many, T., 6

Marshall, K., 26

Marzano, R., 86–87

Marzano's Taxonomy of Objectives, 79

mastery, 145

Mattos, M., 51

McMillan, J. H., 31, 33, 71

McTighe, J., 18

modified assessments, 52

Moon, T., 94

motivation, 144–145

N

Nader, R., 127

Newmann's criteria for Authentic Intellectual Work, 79

Nixon, R. M., 17

nonlearners, intentional, 140

norm-referenced assessments, 22–23

P

performance assessments, 81, 83

personal communication, 83

Pink, D., 144–145

Pixar Animation Studios, 14

Posner, B., 5

post-tests, 93–95

preassessments, 93–94

preparation phase

    assessment maps/plans, 65–68

    components of, 55

    description of, 8–9

    essential learning (priority standards), identifying, 56–60

    learning targets, defining, 60–62

    progress monitoring, 68–69

    SMART goals, establishing, 63–65

    team norms, establishing, 56, 57

pretests, 93–95

priority standards (essential learning), identifying, 56–60

Professional Learning Community at Work™, 6

program improvement

    assessments, 132–135

    components of, 127–128

    curriculum, 129–130

    differentiation, 137–140

    feedback, 150–151, 155–156

    instruction, 130–131

    nonlearners, intentional, 140

response to intervention, 136–137

second-chance testing, 99, 140–142

support between assessments, 142–143

progress monitoring, 68–69

Pryor, J., 85

purpose, 145

R

re-engagement (reteaching), 13–14, 143, 145–149

Reeves, D., 14–15, 58

response to intervention (RTI), 136–137

retesting, 99

Roth, G., 131

S

SAGE Handbook of Research on Classroom Assessment (McMillan), 19, 31

Schneider, C., 19, 29, 91, 118

second-chance testing, 99, 140–142

selected response, 81, 82

Shepard, L., 28, 29, 33

Shim, H. S., 131

singletons, plus one, 49–50

SMART goals, establishing, 63–65

standards, 35–36

  priority standards, identifying, 56–60

Stiggins, R., 32, 61

students with special needs, 50–54

summative assessment, 89–90, 91

T

team assessments, 28–31

team norms, establishing, 56, 57

Tomlinson, C. A., 94

Torrance, H., 85

U

Understanding by Design (Wiggins and McTighe), 18

universal design, 53–54

V

vertical alignment, 40–42

W

Wallace, A., 14

Webb's Depth of Knowledge, 79

Weber, C., 51

whole-school involvement, 37–40

Widder, E., 105

Wiggins, G., 18

Wiliam, D., 21–22, 33, 92, 136

Wright, R., 80

X

Xu, Y., 32, 51

Leading by Design
Cassandra Erkens and Eric Twadell
By focusing on what students learn rather than what they are taught, schools can redefine their mission and begin the transition to a professional learning community. After interviewing and observing principals, administrators, and teachers, the authors identify seven leadership practices that effective PLC leaders share, along with the techniques that have led them to sustainable success.
BKF430

Design in Five
Nicole Dimich Vagle
Fully engage learners in your classroom. Discover how to create high-quality assessments using a five-phase design protocol. Explore types and traits of quality assessment, and learn how to develop assessments that are innovative, effective, and engaging. Evaluate whether your current assessments meet the design criteria, and discover how to use this process collaboratively with your team.
BKF604

Common Formative Assessment
Kim Bailey and Chris Jakicic
Teams that engage in designing, using, and responding to common formative assessments are more knowledgeable about their own standards, more assessment literate, and able to develop more strategies for helping all students learn. In this conversational guide, the authors offer tools, templates, and protocols to incorporate common formative assessments into the practices of a PLC to monitor and enhance student learning.
BKF538

Ahead of the Curve
Edited by Douglas Reeves
This anthology brings the ideas and recommendations of many of the world's education leaders into one resource that illustrates the many perspectives on effective assessment design and implementation. From involving students in the assessment process to ensuring accuracy and applying assessments to English learners and students with special needs, you will find compelling insights and proven strategies.
BKF232

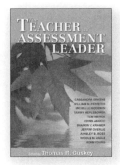

The Teacher as Assessment Leader
Edited by Thomas R. Guskey
Discover how to improve student learning through the power of effective assessment, and realize your power to transform education from inside the classroom. Meaningful examples, expert research, and real-life experiences illustrate the capacity and responsibility every educator has to ignite positive change. Packed with practical strategies from expert practitioners for designing, analyzing, and using assessments, this book shows how to turn best practices into usable solutions.
BKF345

Solution Tree | Press
a division of
Solution Tree

Visit solution-tree.com or call 800.733.6786 to order.

"Excellent engagement
in what truly matters
in **assessment**.

Great examples!"

—Carol Johnson, superintendent,
Central Dauphin School District, Pennsylvania

 PD Services

Our experts draw from decades of research and their own experiences to bring you practical strategies for designing and implementing quality assessments. You can choose from a range of customizable services, from a one-day overview to a multiyear process.

Book your assessment PD today!
888.763.9045

Solution Tree